crime and terrorism

crime and terrorism

Peter Grabosky and Michael Stohl

Los Angeles | London | New Delhi
Singapore | Washington DC

First published 2010

SAGE Publications Ltd
1 Oliver's Yard
55 City Road
London EC1Y 1SP

SAGE Publications Inc.
2455 Teller Road
Thousand Oaks, California 91320

SAGE Publications India Pvt Ltd
B 1/I 1 Mohan Cooperative Industrial Area
Mathura Road
New Delhi 110 044

SAGE Publications Asia-Pacific Pte Ltd
33 Pekin Street #02-01
Far East Square
Singapore 048763

Library of Congress Control Number Available

British Library Cataloguing in Publication data

A catalogue record for this book is available from the British Library

ISBN 978-1-84920-031-8
ISBN 978-1-84920-032-5 (pbk)

Typeset by C&M Digitals (P) Ltd, Chennai, India
Printed by CPI Antony Rowe, Chippenham, Wiltshire
Printed on paper from sustainable resources

contents

acknowledgements

The authors would like to thank Julie Ayling, Sandy Gordon, James Jacobs, and Paul Rock for their comments on an earlier draft, and Christine Nam for her editorial assistance. We are also grateful for the institutional support of the Australian National University's Regulatory Institutions Network, The University of California, Santa Barbara's Department of Communication, Chuo University, and the Australian Research Council Centre of Excellence in Policing and Security.

ONE

introduction: terrorism and terrorists, crime and criminals

Introduction

Organized crime and terrorism are both 'hot button' issues. Not only are they high on the policy agendas of most developed countries, they have become a part of popular culture. But they are not fiction. They can also be real threats to free societies. And, despite their fundamental differences, they have much in common.

This book looks at terrorism through the lens of criminology. In so doing, it seeks to compare two types of illicit activity: terrorism and 'conventional' organized crime. It is surprising, yet understandable, that the explicit comparison of crime (especially organized crime) and terrorism has received relatively little scholarly attention (for exceptions, see Levi, 2006; Morselli, 2009). It is surprising because, as we shall see, terrorism and crime are similar in some respects, as are terrorists and criminals.[1] It is understandable because areas of scholarly inquiry have become increasingly specialized. There are journals and research centers and conferences devoted to organized crime, and others to terrorism, but relatively few combining the two. It is our intention to make a modest contribution towards redressing this imbalance.

---

[1] Terrorism, like crime, is not always organized. Consider the 'London Nail Bomber' and the 'Unabomber,' both of whom appear to have acted alone.

We apologize to those of our readers who are seeking normative guidance, or ideological reinforcement, from this book. While both of us seek a world in which we are optimally free to live our lives, as far as possible free of constraints imposed by terrorists, criminals and the state, we do not propose to mimic a morality play, depicting champions of truth and justice arrayed against forces of evil. Rather, our approach is one of analytical detachment. As you will see, this is easier said than done.

Plan of the book

This chapter will define terrorism and organized crime, and then we explore the degree of overlap of the two. It will then set out a number of theories that provide an explanatory framework for the two types of activity in question. Next we introduce two levels of analysis: the organizational and the individual, with a view towards explaining factors contributing to the genesis, the ascendancy, and the decline of illicit organizations, and the recruitment, the intensification of commitment, and the desistance of individual members.

Chapter 2 summarizes descriptive material on terrorism and organized crime, discussing strengths and weaknesses of available data, and observable trends. It identifies forms of terrorism and of organized crime, and will explore domestic and transnational organized crime as a threat to national and regional security.

Chapter 3 demonstrates that terrorism is hardly the monopoly of political dissidents, but can also be an instrument of political power used by the state. States may engage in terrorism, both domestically and internationally. States may also engage in other forms of criminality, at home and abroad. Chapter 3 also explores the role of corruption, and the links between state actors on the one hand, and criminals and terrorists on the other, and discusses state support for criminal and terrorist activities, both foreign and domestic.

Chapter 4 examines the intersections of terrorist and criminal organizations. Each may engage in similar activity (such as money laundering) to mask their location and activity. They may relate symbiotically, as when they exchange drugs for weapons. Terrorist groups may engage in conventional criminal activity in furtherance of fund raising. Criminal organizations may engage in terrorist activity such as assassination, and can engage in ideologically motivated violence. Chapter 4 also looks at the adaptive behaviour of illicit organizations. The fluid environment within which terrorist and organized crime groups operate provides both threats and opportunities. The development of networked organizational forms by both terrorist and conventional criminal organizations has enhanced both their capacity and their resiliency. Both types of organization exploit emerging technologies, including digital technologies, for use as instruments, targets, or incidentally, for purposes such as record keeping.

Chapter 5 considers state responses to terrorism and to organized crime, and observes notable successes and failures in each domain. In so doing, we discuss the relative merits of 'war fighting' versus criminal justice. We also explore the consequences of strategies that rely on public mobilization, such as the creation of moral panics, and the manipulation of fear. The role of the media in the coverage of crime and terrorism will also be examined.

After a brief summary of the previous chapters, Chapter 6 explores the factors contributing to the decline of terrorist and conventional criminal organizations, and the desistance of their members. We discuss the role of communities and community policing, and offer some conclusions about how to manage organized crime and terrorism effectively, while minimizing encroachments upon human rights and civil liberties.

Definitions

The terms 'crime' and 'terrorism' mean different things to different people. The old adage (however ill-founded) that 'one person's terrorist is another's freedom fighter' hints at this.

In the history of humankind, crime is a relatively modern concept. In prehistoric times, people killed each other, stole each others' property, and did other nasty things. If the victim or victims were strong enough, they responded in a retaliatory manner. Over time, practices of dispute resolution developed, enabling aggrieved parties to seek restitution. Rules of behaviour were unwritten, and what we now refer to as *social control* was informal.

With the passage of time and the corresponding evolution of societies, rules of behaviour became more formal. And so it was that specific acts were prohibited by law, and those who engaged in them became liable to punishment.

The sociologist Richard Quinney (1970) observed that what is deemed to be crime is not frozen in time or place. He is not the first to have done so; Edwin H. Sutherland, for example, made a similar assertion in his and Donald Cressey's *Principles of Criminology*. Crime is a social and political construct. In other words, what is authoritatively and officially defined as crime will vary from time to time and from place to place, depending on social and political circumstances. It may sound somewhat glib to suggest that crime is whatever a government may declare it to be, but this is indeed the case. A few brief examples will illustrate this:

- In 19th century Australia, there existed a thriving whaling industry. Today, it is a criminal offence merely to harass a whale in Australian waters.

- In the People's Republic of China, but nowhere else, it is an offence to advocate the independence of Tibet.

- In the United States, from 1920 to 1933, it was illegal to sell or to purchase an alcoholic beverage. Since then, it has been generally permitted by law, although some cities and counties are still legally 'dry'. There is, of course, a minimum age for the purchase of alcohol, although this too has varied over time and from place to place.

- Citizens of Sweden commit a crime under Swedish law if they pay for sex anywhere in the world – including in Australia, where the sex industry is legal and regulated.

One might suggest that some behaviors, at least in modern times, are universally deemed to be criminal (homicide, for example). But jurisdictions make exceptions in order to excuse homicides occurring in certain circumstances, such as self-defense. And some governments authorize themselves to engage in homicide: as in the execution of criminals. Others condone extrajudicial execution by state authorities. This practice is common in India, and the euphemism used there to refer to deliberate police killings is 'encounters' (Belur 2009).

Organized crime

Organized crime is a term that has been, and continues to be, used very loosely. There are literally scores of definitions of organized crime, and nothing approaching a universal consensus on what it is (see http://www.organized-crime.de/OCDEF1.htm#kvl). Some definitions are based on organizational goals, such as profit. Others focus on the properties of organizations, such as persistence and durability. Some refer to structure (i.e. 'centrally controlled, formal structure') but as we will see, the nature of organizational life is changing, and the criminal organizations that thrived a half century ago bear little resemblance to those that are active today. Other definitions emphasize methods or tools used by organized criminals to achieve their ends, such as violence or bribery. Others still, focus on what some criminal organizations do, such as drug trafficking and loan sharking. For our purposes, we shall refer to organized crime as criminal activity by groups of three or more individuals who engage in criminal activities collaboratively, with a degree of structure and coordination.

Terrorism

Terrorism, too, can be a slippery term. The definition of terrorism that we prefer is the following: 'An act or threat of *violence* to create *fear* and/or *compliant behavior* in a *victim* or wider *audience* for the purpose of achieving *political ends*' (Stohl, 1988: 3; emphasis added. The words are key to understanding terrorism).

A number of terrorist groups in various locations around the globe have been active since the turn of the century. Most prominent among these are the various Islamic fundamentalist groups such as the Taliban in Afghanistan and Pakistan, Al Qaeda in the Middle East, Lashkar-e-Taiba in Pakistan, Jamaa Islamiya (JI) in Indonesia, and Abu Sayyaf in the Philippines. Until their demise in 2009, the Liberation Tigers of Tamil Eelam sought independence from Sri Lanka. In Europe, the Irish Republican Army and its offshoots have been less active since the 9/11 attacks created a hostile environment for political violence in western democracies.

Similarly the Basque separatist group ETA declared a permanent ceasefire in 2006, although occasional violent incidents were recorded in 2009.

Of course, terrorism existed long before September 11, 2001; classical and biblical references abound. And one should note that the acts in question need not exclusively be the work of individuals or dissident groups. Indeed, the very term terrorism emerged in the aftermath of the French Revolution to refer to the repressive practices of the state. The Soviet Union during the Stalin era (1922–53), and Germany under Hitler (1933–45), were terrorist states. State terrorism can also occur across national frontiers. The 1983 bombing of visiting South Korean officials in Rangoon was the work of North Korean government agents. Libyan government operatives were responsible for the bombing of an airliner (Pan Am 103) over Lockerbie, Scotland in 1988. French secret service agents sank the Greenpeace vessel Rainbow Warrior in Auckland Harbour in July 1985. Pakistan has sponsored terrorist attacks in Indian Kashmir.

Most if not all acts of terrorism entail some type of crime. An act or threat of violence is an assault – an offence at common law. Such acts that inflict loss of life are, of course, homicides. Malicious damage to property, regardless of motive, is a crime almost anywhere. So why then do states enact specific laws that make terrorism a crime? We will revisit this question briefly at the end of this chapter, and again in Chapter 5.

The crime–terror interface

As we will see in subsequent chapters, terrorism and organized crime may overlap, and their protagonists may occupy the same playing field (Makarenko, 2004). The intersection of crime and terrorism may take the following forms:

- Terrorists may engage in conventional criminality to support themselves and their operations. Al Qaeda has engaged in credit card fraud; Abu Sayyaf in ransom kidnapping. Profits from cigarette smuggling in the United States have gone to support Hezbollah.

- Organized criminals may seek to coerce and intimidate governments and their citizens for political ends. The assassinations of Sicilian investigating judges

Giovanni Falcone and Paolo Borsellino in 1992 were more than just Mafia 'hits,' the massive explosions themselves constituted a political statement, and were obviously intended to discourage further investigative activity.

- Ordinary criminals may become increasingly politicized, and eventually convert to terrorism. Jose Padilla, a US citizen convicted after 9/11 of aiding terrorists, was, in his youth, a member of a Chicago street gang. Mohammed Bouyeri, the assassin of Dutch filmmaker Theo van Gogh, was a petty criminal before he turned to political violence in 2004.

- Terrorists may abandon their political agendas and turn to conventional crime (Rosenthal, 2008). The term 'fighters turned felons' (Curtis and Karacan, 2002) captures this nicely. One of the largest bank robberies in UK history was allegedly committed to finance the retirement of IRA activists in 2004 following the peace accords in Northern Ireland.

- Terrorist and criminal organizations may exchange knowledge and commodities for mutual benefit. Southern Thai criminals sell weapons to insurgents. Mincheva and Gurr (2010) refer to 'marriages of convenience' such as the relationship between the Revolutionary Armed Forces of Colombia (FARC) and Colombian drug dealers. JI in Indonesia literally married into the criminal class, with a senior member marrying a major arms merchant to ensure continuing supply of arms.

- Some hybrid organizations may engage in both terrorist and criminal activity. The Indian organized crime syndicate D-Company is alleged to have been involved in drug trafficking, money laundering, and a bombing in Mumbai that killed 257 people in 1993.

The crime–terror interface is not new, but it has certainly received a lot of attention lately. The term 'Narco-terrorism' was coined as far back as the 1980s to describe some of the tactics of Latin American drug cartels. The Nicaraguan Contras engaged in cocaine trafficking to support their insurgency at roughly the same time (see Cohen, 1996).

Some controversy surrounds the issue of convergence: whether those terrorists who take on criminal traits for purposes of terrorism (either to commit the terrorist act or support themselves from day to day) actually *become* criminals – and vice versa. There are two schools of thought in this debate. One, involving Stern (2003: 215, 251),

Makarenko (2004) and Dishman (2005), argues that convergence does exist and can remain permanent. The other, involving Schmid (1996) and Hutchinson and O'Malley (2007) argues that terrorism and crime are very different in their motivations and that therefore convergence is at best very infrequent. To the extent that interaction takes place, it is simply an alliance of convenience.

Theories

One of the goals of social science is to develop an explanatory framework that will enable us to understand changes over time in social and political phenomena – in this case organized crime, and terrorism. Our analysis will embrace four theoretical perspectives. The most comprehensive will be what criminologists call routine activity theory. We will also draw upon differential association theory and strain theory to explain the behaviour of individual criminals and terrorists. Finally, we will seek to explain the behaviour of criminal and terrorist organizations in terms of resource dependency theory.

Routine activity theory

One of the most useful criminological theories, developed by Cohen and Felson (1979) is called routine activity theory. In essence, a terrorist act, or crime in general, may be explained by the conjunction of three factors: 1) a supply of motivated offenders; 2) the availability of suitable targets or victims, and 3) the absence of capable guardianship (in other words, surveillance, vigilance, or someone to 'mind the store').

1 Motives

A simplistic comparison of the motives driving organized criminals with those that inspire terrorists would suggest that organized criminals are in it for the money and that people become terrorists because they want to change the world (or at least their small part of it). Conventional criminal organizations are business organizations; terrorist groups are political organizations. This may be true, but only to a point. Life is complex, and individuals are rarely driven by a single objective. Motives for criminal or terrorist activity, or for antisocial behavior in general, are varied. Both criminals and terrorists may harbor a number of these.

The most common of these motives are greed, lust, rebellion, indignation, and the desire for personal security, power, revenge, excitement, or respect. In some cases, intellectual challenge may also come into play. Outsmarting a powerful adversary may be gratifying in itself.

Chu (2000) describes how many Chinese would join a triad gang for personal protection, in much the same way kids in Chicago or Los Angeles would join a street gang. One official attributed the attraction of the Philippine terrorist group Abu Sayyaf to 'religion, thrills and joblessness' (quoted in Rosenthal, 2008: 64).

The exercise of power may at times entail humiliation. Videotaped messages from Osama bin Laden were intended not only to create fear, but also to generate support among potential sympathizers and to demean the United States and its allies.

The desire for status and respect is also an important motivator. Both organized crime and terrorist groups may attract 'nobodies who want to be somebody.' Paoli (2003: 83) refers to members of the Sicilian Mafia holding 'strong feelings of superiority to the external world.'[2] By no means unique to terrorists or organized criminals, this explanation may apply also to those who join the navy, the police, or indeed, those who become university academics. But one can appreciate the attraction, especially for someone from fairly ordinary circumstances, of the fast life of the underworld, or joining the vanguard of a revolution or holy war.

---

[2]The original Mafiosi *were* somebody – people charged with management and enforcement duties in Sicilian estates with absentee landlords (see Blok, 1975). Gambetta (1996) sees the essence and genesis of the Mafia in 'the business of private protection.' With the decline of the feudal age, where interpersonal trust was generally lacking, the Mafia emerged to provide services of social control and conflict resolution. By contrast, Blok (1975) saw the Mafia as 'violent entrepreneurs' shielding the landed aristocracy from the rising peasantry and the emerging Italian state. While their explanations for the emergence of the Mafia diverge, both recognize the embedded nature of the emergence in the relationship between the community and the external world and the organization's ability to provide a 'service' to the local community in the form of more reliable protection than that provided by the state or aristocracy.

Sageman (2008) suggests that glory may be a motivating factor behind suicide terrorism. The attraction of joining a powerful and (in the eyes of some) prestigious entity may also come into play. Other factors might include clan loyalties, perceptions of historic injustices and revenge.

One of the more distinctive, if not unique, motivating factors for terrorists is moral outrage (Sageman, 2008: 57). Here it is important to note that the perception of injustice, and the attribution of responsibility for injustice, need not be widely shared. It is often the intensity of the perception and attribution that matters. Consider Timothy McVeigh, whose contempt for what he regarded as a tyrannical US federal government, and whose outraged indignation over the 1993 siege in Waco Texas, resulted exactly two years later in the bombing of the Murrah Federal Building in Oklahoma City. In his study of suicide terrorists, Pape (2005) identified the common factor of indignation over the occupation of one's homeland by foreign forces. In the wired world of the 21st century, where the global has become the local, it is not necessary to be directly confronted by occupying forces in order to become very angry. Images of Guantanamo, or of women's and children's bodies in Iraq, may be enough to mobilize hatred and to inspire action on that sentiment if one identifies with the victims. As Innes et al. (2007) observe, even lesser slights, occurring closer to home, may create an environment for festering grievances. Personal or vicarious exposure to hate crime or discrimination may entail lasting damage. Perceived local injustice may be intensified by perceived global injustice, and vice versa.

A great deal of criminal and terrorist activity is the work of groups rather than lone individuals. The collective nature of illicit activity may also bear upon individual motives. In particular, the desire for fraternity, camaraderie or fellowship can be an important factor in explaining why one joins a criminal gang, or a terrorist group. This can be particularly significant in modern pluralistic societies where migrants or members of ethnic or religious minorities may feel excluded from the dominant culture. It is a natural tendency for individuals in these circumstances to seek out similarly situated people with whom they can identify. Illicit organizations, whether criminal or terrorist, may provide such fraternity.

2 Opportunities

The second pillar of routine activity theory is the availability of suitable targets or victims. Organized criminals seek out opportunities to provide illicit goods and/or services for profit. Where prostitution, drugs, and gambling are illegal, criminal organizations are usually active. They may also engage in extortion, and loan sharking (providing credit at exorbitant rates of interest). In some places, criminal organizations may infiltrate legitimate businesses, either to use them as fronts for illegal activity or to strip their assets.

Opportunities for terrorists are nearly everywhere. Any significant concentration of people, core societal institutions (governmental, financial) or critical infrastructure (transport, communications, water and power supplies) can make an attractive target. Prominent monuments or buildings may have particular symbolic value, as did the Pentagon and the World Trade Center in 2001.

You can see that it would be difficult to reduce the number of prospective targets for terrorists. Doing away with air travel in order to prevent aircraft hijacking is simply not an option. Strategies of opportunity reduction therefore tend to entail what is called 'target hardening' – making a target less accessible or more resistant to attack. Thus, the fortification of cockpit doors in commercial aircraft and the reduction of easy access to many public buildings and sites. In Washington, D.C., it is no longer possible to drive along Pennsylvania Avenue past the White House. These new traffic arrangements place the building beyond the reach of truck bombers.

3 Guardians

Criminals or terrorists are less likely to act if they suspect that someone may be watching. Police cannot be everywhere, however, and recent years have seen enormous growth in institutions of surveillance. Cash transactions reporting agencies have been created in order to identify the proceeds of crime, and more recently, sources of terrorist finance. The private security sector has expanded dramatically in most industrial nations, to the extent that private security guards outnumber police by two or three times. Of course in poorer countries, private security guards protect the rich from the poor because the public sector does not have the resources. In both rich countries and poor we create gated communities.

Surveillance can be enhanced by technological means. The use of metal detectors to screen airline passengers has been around for nearly half a century. Today, surveillance cameras are seemingly everywhere. Credit card companies have developed sophisticated computer programs to analyze credit card use and to identify unusual patterns of spending that may be indicative of theft or fraud. And the use of telecommunications interception against organized criminals and terrorists has become widespread.

Differential association theory

Another theory of criminal and terrorist motivation is the theory of *Differential Association*. Introduced by the eminent American criminologist Edwin Sutherland (1947), differential association theory suggests that people learn from those with whom they 'hang out.' They reinforce each others' inclinations.

The term 'family' to refer to some organized crime groups is not misplaced. Because trust is such an important consideration between collaborating criminals and terrorists, particularly when they cannot rely on the resources of civil society, they are often recruited with care. A relative is usually a known quantity, and family bonds may be stronger than the ties formed from mere acquaintances.

Social ties may develop elsewhere than in the family or on the street corner. They may be forged in prison, or on the battlefield. Shared experiences and the mutual trust that develops in prison may serve as the basis for collaboration in legitimate, or illegitimate, activities upon release. Similarly, interpersonal bonds forged in combat may also support subsequent collaboration. Those combatants who resisted the Soviet occupation of Afghanistan in the 1980s returned to fight the United States two decades later. A number of individuals who were engaged in hostilities following the dissolution of Yugoslavia formed criminal gangs once peace was restored (Glenny, 2008).

Differential association may also be enhanced by shared experience of what Martin Innes (2004) would refer to as 'signal events.' These are incidents, usually of an adverse nature, that galvanize public attention. They may have been shared directly and personally, as the experience of discrimination, or they may be experienced vicariously, as when the images of abuse in Abu Ghraib prison were widely publicized.

Strain theory

Another theory of motivation that can be used to explain both criminal and terrorist activity is Merton's strain theory. In essence, Merton (1938) observed that criminal or terrorist activity will take place when the individual's goals are unattainable by legitimate means.

The person who covets a Ferrari but who cannot afford one may become a drug dealer; the individual residing in a land governed by an oppressive and unaccommodating colonial power may resort to terrorist activity in furtherance of national liberation. Strain should not be acquainted with economic disadvantage. Sageman's (2008; 48) systematic study of contemporary terrorists revealed that a large majority came from middle class backgrounds. One can be relatively comfortable in a material sense, but still feel profoundly disempowered. Umar Farouk Abdulmutallah, who was charged with the attempted bombing of an airliner in December 2009, came from one of the wealthiest families in Nigeria.

Resource dependency theory

Resource dependency theory holds that organizations obtain resources essential to their survival and growth by establishing relations with outside entities (Pfeffer and Salancik, 1978). In the first instance, they may be dependent upon these external actors. Ultimately the organization will seek to make external actors dependent upon it. This will become apparent in our discussion of the relationships of terrorist groups and conventional criminal organizations to their social environment. The relationship may range from the predatory, where the organization exercises coercive power over its neighbors, or symbiotic, where the relationship is mutually advantageous to the organization and its surrounding constituents.

Organizations require resources in order to survive. These resources can be material, such as guns, explosives, or the cash with which to buy them. Resources can be less tangible, but no less important. A degree of community support can make or break an organization. Recall Chairman Mao's dictum about the guerilla relating to the people as the fish swims in the ocean. Recall the downfall of Che Guevara, who was unsuccessful in winning the hearts and minds of the Bolivian peasantry. The success of a terrorist or organized crime group may depend on its ability to garner and maintain resources.

Governments, for their part, seek to recover proceeds of crime and to interdict terrorist financing. They also devote considerable effort to producing propaganda, with a view towards turning public opinion against illicit organizations.

Levels of analysis

One useful way of comparing organized crime and terrorism is to focus on two levels of analysis: the organizational and the individual. At the organizational level, one may compare the genesis, ascendancy and decline of the two organizational types – specifically the factors that brought them into being, those that explain their institutionalization, and those that contributed to their demise.

Explanatory factors can be properties of the organization itself – its size, structure, and so on, or they can be factors that reside in the organization's environment. Environmental factors can include the presence or absence of competitors; the degree of community support for the organization and its goals, and the capacity or willingness of the state to control the organization. Such support can fluctuate in complex fashion – in response to external threat, for example (see Burton, 1978).

At the individual level, one may seek to explain the recruitment of individual members, their intensification of commitment (or radicalization), and their eventual desistance (departure from the organization). Explanatory factors might include personal psychological characteristics; social factors such as class background and peer group; and situational or historical factors. While many assume that particular psychological profiles may be associated with criminal or terrorist recruitment, there is little evidence that this is the case (see Merari, 2005; Rausch, 1979). Many surviving members of the French resistance during World War II returned to fairly ordinary lives after Liberation from Nazi occupation. Those members of conventional criminal groups who grow old on the job may finish their days on the golf course. Some outlaw motorcycle gangs even have by-laws relating to retirement (Mallory, 2007: 167). The Japanese government has arranged for vocational counseling and job placement services for former members of Yakuza organizations (Fujimoto, 1998).

1 Organizational genesis

Conventional criminal organizations come into being to exploit criminal opportunities. These opportunities may arise from:

- The unwillingness or inability of the state to provide institutions of social control and/or conflict resolution. Both Blok (1975) and Gambetta (1996) describe how, during the formation of the Italian state in the 19th century, certain areas of the country lacked access to legal institutions that could provide for the enforcement of contracts. Criminal organizations emerged to meet this need. Even today, in many places around the world, criminal organizations provide 'protection' for a fee.

- A public demand for illicit goods and services. Where jurisdictions prohibit such things as drugs, gambling, commercial sex, or the movement of people across national borders, criminals are often available to supply these goods and services on a commercial basis. The enactment of Prohibition in the United States presented organized criminals with truly golden opportunities.

- The vulnerability of legitimate enterprises to exploitation by criminals. Criminal organizations may infiltrate an otherwise legal enterprise. It was once said that 'the best way to rob a bank is to own one.' (Black, 2005). Russian organized criminals would no doubt agree. In the 20th century, a number of trade unions in the US fell under Mafia control, and their pension funds were siphoned off (Jacobs, 2006). Organized criminals may also take advantage of certain supply chain or market vulnerabilities for purposes of extortion. Time-critical processes, such as the delivery of concrete to a construction site, may invite organized criminals to threaten delay unless payment is made (Goldstock et al., 1990).

By contrast, terrorist groups tend to come into being as a result of intense political grievances. Such grievances may arise because of perceived historical, economic, social or political injustices and need not be rational and justifiable to outsiders, or widely shared. What matters is their intensity. The grievances may be sharply focused, such as the presence of foreign occupying forces. They may, on the other hand, be quite diffuse and even apocalyptic, as was the case with the Aum sect in Japan, which sought to destroy the world in order to save it. What also matters is that the person suffering the grievance has little prospect of redress through the current political system; terrorism is typically a tool of the weak.

2 Organizational ascendancy

The structure of illicit organizations can be instrumental to their sustainability. The traditional way of perceiving criminal organizations, and some terrorist groups, was to regard them as monolithic, hierarchical and pyramidal in nature. To some extent, this image was derived from the apparent structure of traditional Mafia organizations in Sicily and in North America. While this may have been an accurate representation at an earlier historical period, this is no longer the case. Organizational life, both licit and illicit, has changed dramatically in the past quarter century. Large hierarchies are being replaced, or coexist with decentralized networks, or by loose coalitions (Hobbs, 2001).

Kenney (2007) contends that Al Qaeda and Colombian drug organizations share flat decision making hierarchies. They tend to be compartmented networks, rather than hierarchies. Far from a vertically integrated enterprise, where production, transportation, wholesale distribution, and retailing are all done by the same organization, drug traffic is the work of many independent enterprises that may be described as loosely coupled chain networks. He argues that Al Qaeda has further transformed from a loose network to an amorphous movement: 'more of an ideology than a locus of decision making authority' (Kenney, 2007: 11). In this view of the organization it is no longer even a franchise. Islamic militancy has become a state of mind, its practitioners operating independently. There is no need to communicate with Osama bin Laden, wherever he may be (we will discuss further this type of organization in Chapter 4, and will refer to the persistence of nodes in settings such as madrassas, mosques and tribes).

As we will observe, this type of organizational structure has significant implications for strategies of interdiction. The death or arrest of a movement leader may have symbolic value for law enforcement and security agencies, but it may have little impact on the illicit organization's activities at the grass roots. Indeed, it may have symbolic value there as well, if the leader is perceived as a kind of hero.

3 Organizational decline

Illicit organizations may wither and die for a number of reasons. They may be suppressed by the state, or by competing illicit organizations. They may otherwise fail to adapt to a changing organizational environment.

'Wars' between and among organized crime groups can be extremely debilitating. They may arise from competition for market share, or from perceived disrespect for another's leaders or members. More generally, they may arise because there are no institutionalized methods of dispute resolution. Once they commence, these conflicts can result in a spiral of violence and retaliation.

Needless to say, organizational behaviour can be driven by combinations of factors. Jacobs describes the decline of the New York Mafia as having resulted from aggressive enforcement by the state, including extensive investigation based on telecommunications interception. They were also challenged by some very aggressive newcomers, from places like Jamaica and Russia. In addition, Jacobs noted that the children of Mafia leaders often chose to pursue legitimate professional careers, rather than join the family business.

Paoli (2003) describes the lack of adaptability on the part of Sicilian Mafia groups: among the factors she identifies are the inward focus on family, village and neighborhood, the inability or unwillingness to broaden the pool of new recruits, and the consequent failure to exploit emerging opportunities such as the growing illicit arms trade.

Another important variable that may explain an illicit organization's viability is its relationship with the community within which it resides. The degree of community support may be crucial. This is hardly a new idea; the legend of Robin Hood goes back a long way. At play here is the state's own ability or capacity to meet the needs of its citizens.

In Oakland, California during the 1960s, members of the Black Panther Party provided free breakfasts to local children. In the immediate aftermath of the Kobe Earthquake in 1995, members of Yamaguchi-Gumi, Japan's largest criminal organization, distributed blankets and drinking water to the homeless. In southern Lebanon today, Hezbollah and Hamas, respectively, perform a significant welfare role. Of course, Hamas has also been elected to government in Gaza.

The community relations function of an illicit organization need not be undertaken with the aim of recruiting new members. Passive or active support, or simply tolerance, may have considerable value to an organization.[3] Third parties may also contribute to a climate of support for an illicit organization. In the northwest of Pakistan, when governments were no longer in a position to provide free education and began charging fees, madrassas were established to serve those children whose parents could not afford to send their children to state schools. The religious education received may well have contributed to their support for militant groups.

More than ever before, the world is a rapidly changing place. Criminal opportunities emerge and disappear. Developments in technology may provide new instruments of crime. States may enhance, or relax their vigilance or reactive capacity. Competitors may energetically seek a bigger market share. The organization that understands the environment in which it operates, and structures itself accordingly, is more likely to survive in the long run. Those organizations that carry on business as usual will become the dinosaurs of crime or terrorism, and will eventually find themselves extinct.

Kenney (2007) focuses on just this issue – the adaptability of illicit organizations (for earlier discussions, see Hall, 1935 and McIntosh, 1975). The essence of Kenney's argument is that successful organized criminal groups and terrorist organizations are 'learning organizations' that adapt successfully to ecological stresses. Kenney refers to the struggle between the illicit organization and the state as 'competitive adaptation.' Learning organizations engage in their own research and development. Kenney further notes that the best drug traffickers engage in significant research and experimentation. For example, when it became increasingly difficult for cocaine traffickers to land their product directly in the United States using light aircraft, they began to develop techniques of delivery through airdrops at sea to small boats which might reach the mainland unobtrusively (2007: 50). This entailed 'trial runs' (using flour rather than cocaine) to determine the optimal size of consignment, altitude for release, and the most appropriate wrapping.

---

[3]It may also be a powerful part of a vocabulary of motive or technique of neutralization. See Landesco's (1968) chapter on the gangster's *apologia pro vita sua.*

Astute criminal organizations also analyze law enforcement techniques through close reading of court documents (2007: 72).

Improvements in the lethality of improvised explosive devices and 'roadside bombs' are unlikely to occur by chance. Rather, they too tend to reflect processes of trial and error, and progressive refinement.

Changes in organizational form may occur in response to successful enforcement efforts. Kenney (2007: 217) observed that as major cocaine networks were interdicted, Colombia's illicit drug industry became decentralized. After Al Qaeda was evicted from Afghanistan, its operations decentralized, to the extent that it is now often characterized as a movement rather than an organization in the traditional sense.

Leadership

The quality of leadership may be crucial to an organization's viability. A charismatic leader may attract recruits and may sustain commitment by members of the organization during difficult times. An organization that depends too much on charismatic leadership may, however, suffer the consequences if the leader is removed. Leaders themselves may contribute to this. To the extent that they encourage the development of a 'cult of personality,' there may be no one to replace them in the event that they are neutralized by death or capture.

Decapitation of an organization by removal of a charismatic leader may lead to organizational decline. Alternatively, it may create a martyr, a powerful rallying symbol, and thereby lead to an organizational rejuvenation. Organizational structure may also determine the impact of the loss of a charismatic leader; horizontal network forms of organization are more resistant to such losses than are vertical traditional organizational hierarchies.

Individual level explanations

Recruitment

There are both similarities and differences in the background of terrorists and organized criminals. The latter tend to come from relatively disadvantaged backgrounds, in which opportunities for social and financial advancement by legitimate means tend to be limited (unless, of course, you include corporate criminals). By contrast, many terrorists (as do other political radicals, violent and non-violent) come from mainstream backgrounds. The Aum Shinrikyo sect contained many professionals, including scientists and engineers (Lifton, 2000). Many members of the Baader-Meinhof group were distinctly middle class. More recently, systematic studies of Islamic terrorists have shown them also to have been drawn from middle-class backgrounds, with an overrepresentation of engineers and physicians (Sageman, 2008). Osama bin Laden himself, of course, came from a background of exceptional wealth.

Illicit organizations may be born of shared experience. In the case of both organized crime and terrorism, this can occur on the streets, or in prison. In the case of terrorism, it can occur on the battlefield. We noted earlier how triad gangs attract recruits who regard themselves at risk of victimization at the hands of any gangs should they remain unaffiliated.

One of the most fertile recruiting grounds for illicit organizations is prison. Here, imprisoned gang members may seek out new members from their fellow inmates, who literally constitute a captive audience. The recruitment pitch may be coercive, it may entail positive reinforcement, or it can involve both. Personal security is even more at risk in prison than on the street. Illicit organizations may also arise from repeated interactions among prisoners with no previous organizational affiliations. With a great deal of time on their hands, these individuals may plan further criminality of a collective nature after their release.

Terrorists may also be recruited in prison. Where a terrorist movement has a spiritual theme, religious services in prison may provide the forum for militants to proselytize.

The battlefield will also provide an opportunity for terrorist recruitment. Friendships forged under fire may evolve into continued relationships in furtherance of a cause. Coll (2004) describes how the Afghan resistance, formed to resist the Soviet occupation of Afghanistan in 1979, established the social bonds that eventually provided the basis for Al Qaeda. This was also true in the 1950s as returned Algerian soldiers in the French colonial army in Vietnam were recruited into the National Liberation Front (FLN) in the cause of Algerian independence (see Horne, 1977; Crenshaw, 1978).

Intensification of commitment

Pre-existing friendship and kinship networks have also been observed to be avenues of socialization for both terrorist and conventional criminal organizations. The four preconditions for radicalization observed by Innes and his colleagues (2007) in relation to Islamic militancy in the UK include:

- *Inter*-community separation, where a minority group is unwilling or unable to integrate into mainstream society;

- *Intra*-community separation, where alienated members create a 'minority within a minority' and withdraw from the wider minority community;

- Ideology, which reinforces the individual's indignation and suggests a path to redressing their grievances; and

- Group dynamics, where individuals reinforce each other's attitudes and inclinations.

One of the greatest threats to an organization's survival is attrition of membership. Members must be recruited and retained. If they disengage, whether in the line of duty or through desertion, the knowledge they take with them may jeopardize the entire organization. So early on in an individual's career, he or she will experience measures to 'lock them in.'

Illicit organizations of an extremely diverse nature manifest similar patterns of behaviour designed to intensify commitment. In her book on the Sicilian Mafia, Paoli (2003) observes the symbols and rituals designed to cement members within the organization. Initiation ceremonies, based on a blood oath, are intended to achieve the functional equivalent of a religious conversion (for a discussion of rites of passage, see van Gennep, 1909). Lest there be any doubt of lifetime commitment, recruits are advised, 'One goes in and comes out of Cosa Nostra with blood. You will see for yourselves, in a little while, how one enters with blood. And if you leave, you'll leave with blood because you'll be killed' (Arlacchi and Calderone, 1992: 68). Chinese triads are remarkably similar. Morgan (1960; 157–160) describes a traditional triad initiation which included the oath: 'If I should change my mind and deny my membership of the Hung family, I will be killed by a myriad of swords.'

The Aum Sect sought to discourage members from leaving by kidnapping and torturing those who tried. The Mau Mau movement in Kenya in the 1950s resorted to blood oaths and secret bonding ceremonies.

One question of great interest to both scholars and policy makers today concerns the intensification of commitment of new or prospective members of illicit organizations. The term 'radicalization' is commonly used to refer to would-be terrorists. There appears to be no standard 'recipe' or developmental path for radicalization. Innes et al. (2007: 11) refer to a 'range of additive factors' that may occur 'in different combinations and sequences for different individuals.'

Referring to Muslim youth in England, Innes observed feelings of anomie and disconnection – a kind of alienation from mainstream British society. This search for identity and meaning is by no means limited to the experience of Muslims in western society. Lifton (2000) observed how alienation of young professionals in Japan led them to the Aum Shinrikyo, the quasi-religious cult that sought to achieve a new world order by using weapons of mass destruction.

The IRA socialized members through an increasing escalation of sophisticated violent operations culminating in a 'passing out ceremony.' The individual thereby becomes bound to the cause by act of outlawry (Kenney, 2007: 142).

Desistance and disengagement

Desistance from criminal or disengagement from terrorist activity may take different paths. Arrest and death in the line of duty are occupational hazards of both types of organization. By definition, suicide terrorism entails individual desistance. The extensive literature on desistance from conventional criminal activity has been summarized in two major reviews (Laub and Sampson, 2001; Kazemian and Farrington, 2007).

Traditional delinquency tends to peak in late adolescence and decline gradually thereafter. This applies to members of youth gangs, as well as to individual offenders. Most young offenders develop improved capacities of rational decision making and self-control that lead them along a more law-abiding path. Many develop romantic and/or vocational interests that distract them from peers who would otherwise lead them astray. And the peers themselves may experience similar lifestyle changes. It is not surprising that the influence of one's peer group is important to both the onset and the desistance of conventional criminality. Differential association is a powerful theory.

For those who choose to engage in illicit organizational activity as adults, other factors may contribute to desistance. Depending on how arduous criminal or terrorist work (and the imprisonment that may, from time to time, accompany it) may be, or the individual's belief in the chances of future success (see Ross and Gurr, 1989), the person in question may just 'burn out.' If they see themselves as exploited or shortchanged by leaders of the organization, they may (despite the risks noted above) be tempted to abdicate. In some cases, they may be tempted to turn against their fellow members and offer to assist the state. The decision may be made easier by the availability of witness protection programs, which can offer the 'deserter' a new identity in a new location or the encouragement of the community from which they have come.

Information flows within and between organizations

Both illicit organizations and the governments wishing to control them possess information that, for obvious reasons, they want to keep secret. As a result, they tend to compartmentalize information. When an illicit organization does this, it trades off knowledge for security (Kenney, 2007: 5). The same principle applies to counterterrorist organizations. Kenney refers to 'the necessary tension between concealment and coordination.' Morselli et al. (2007) refer to the 'efficiency–security tradeoff.'

When law enforcement agencies compartmentalize information, they may do so for legitimate reasons of security. After all, there have been a number of prominent cases involving senior officials of the FBI and CIA who have sold or otherwise shared information with targets and adversaries. Kim Philby, a senior official of the British Secret Intelligence Service (MI6), was in fact a Soviet agent. But impediments to information flow do not always have a legitimate justification. Many law enforcement officials are acutely sensitive to their own personal or institutional self-interest. In law enforcement, as in other areas of public administration, much of life is about gaining and preserving 'turf.' By sharing sensitive information with another law enforcement agency, one risks the possibility that the information might go astray, or that the recipient of the information will use it for his or her advantage, without even acknowledging its provenance. The legendary rivalry between the FBI and the CIA before the attacks on September 11, 2001 was accompanied by very poor communication between the two agencies, as was noted by the 9/11 Commission (National Commission on Terrorist Attacks upon the United States, 2004).

Another informal impediment to information flow within organizations, at least when the information entails bad news, is the risk that the recipient may react by 'shooting the messenger.' This has the effect of distorting the information that is transmitted upwards within an organization, so that good news is amplified, and bad news, if it is transmitted at all, is muted. One can appreciate the challenges this poses to decision makers who genuinely seek the best available evidence on which to base a course of action.

There are obvious risks inherent in impeding information flow. Balancing them against the risks of wider disclosure is a formidable challenge.

State response

States and cultures have their own ways of defining problems and of responding to them. In the United States, the metaphor of war is commonly used to describe state response to major issues. Thus, one saw the War on Poverty during the Johnson Administration, Nixon's War on Drugs, and most recently, during the George W Bush administration, the War on Terror.

The implications of this are not merely rhetorical. Conventional 'shooting wars' have tended to be accompanied by considerable secrecy and misinformation. One recalls the aphorism, 'The first casualty when war comes is truth.' Wars also tend to be accompanied by significant curtailment of civil liberties, especially freedom to question the wisdom of going to war in the first place, and freedom to challenge the way in which hostilities are being managed. Wars can also entail gross mistreatment of an adversary – combatants and non-combatants alike. And finally, wars are financially very costly. They tend to require extensive spending on weaponry, often at the expense of careful cost/benefit calculation and to the detriment of other programs and policies. This is not to suggest that such sacrifices are unwarranted. Indeed, a nation's survival may depend upon them. What we are suggesting is that wherever possible, one should not only choose their wars carefully but also carefully choose what is labeled as a war.

State responses to the threat or the reality of terrorism tend to entail a flurry of legislation. Governments enact legislation with special reference to terrorism for a number of reasons:

First, governments may seek to demonstrate to the citizenry that they are not standing idly by in the face of a terrorist threat, but that they are doing something about it. Redundancy in legislation is not always a bad thing or a waste of lawmakers' time.

Second, they may enact special terrorism legislation in order to increase penalties available to impose on convicted terrorists, and thereby send a message to the judiciary that the state regards terrorism as a particularly serious form of crime.

Third, they may enact special terrorism legislation to facilitate the enhancement of special powers of surveillance, investigation, search and seizure. These are intrusive enforcement tools that might not ordinarily be justified.

They may also enact legislation for purposes of prevention – to make it more difficult to prepare for a terrorist act by communicating for the purposes of recruitment and planning, or by acquiring certain materials that might be used in furtherance of an attack.

Governments also enact legislation to facilitate cooperation under the principle of like crime in different jurisdictions. For example, UN Resolution 1373 urges countries to criminalize terrorist financing and related activities.

As Chapter 5 will suggest, this may require carefully crafted legislation if it is not to infringe human rights, especially freedom of speech and association. You will also see in Chapter 5 that countries may enact specialized legislation directed against organized crime, for many of the same reasons.

Ironies of state response to terrorism and organized crime

Despite their fundamentally adversarial relationship, illicit organizations and those of the state may at times assist each other.

States may at times rely directly or indirectly upon illicit organizations to serve their own ends. Organized criminals were instrumental in discouraging labor unrest on the New York waterfront during World War II. As part of its persistent but unsuccessful efforts to assassinate Fidel Castro, the Kennedy Administration enlisted the support of the Mafia. McCoy (1972) observed that the CIA collaborated with drug traffickers in Laos and Burma throughout most of the Cold War. The US military under President Bush employed the services of the notorious arms dealer Victor Bout to deliver weapons to Iraq from 2003–2005 (Farrah and Braun, 2007).

When states pronounce an illicit organization to be a 'bête noire' they risk conferring a status on the illicit organization that may unintentionally attract public support. The legendary Ned Kelly and his gang, famous outlaws of 19th century Australia, became national icons. Illich Ramirez Sanchez, aka 'Carlos the Jackal' became a media celebrity in the 1970s as the world's most glamorous terrorist rather than a killer for hire. When an organization or its leadership achieves celebrity status, members of the public may become tolerant if not celebratory. The term 'radical chic' served as part of the title of a famous book by Tom Wolfe (1970) which referenced the Black Panthers and their interaction with New York 'high society.' The term 'gangster chic' has been used in Australia recently to refer to underworld celebrities. Ironically, to be identified as the embodiment of evil may redound to a group's benefit.

Organizations tend not to be satisfied with the status quo, and usually covet more resources and more power. Law enforcement and security agencies are no exception. By accentuating the risk of crime and or terrorism, these agencies, and the governments that they represent, may seek to justify increased resources.

Governments may also identify and emphasize threats for political purposes. They may wish to distract attention from other problems. They may wish to create an enemy for the purpose of rallying support from the public. They may wish to be seen to be acting, confidently and assertively, to address a problem. And they may wish to demonstrate that their political adversaries are no match for the government in terms of their willingness and ability to confront the enemy.

Aspiring politicians, or upwardly mobile political officials, may seek to generate political capital by emphasizing their achievements in crime fighting or counter-terrorism. Former New York Mayor Rudolph Giuliani is one prominent example of a politician who portrayed himself as a hero in both domains.

Terrorist groups may seek to provoke the state into introducing extremely repressive measures, thereby alienating the public. To the extent that the state plays into the terrorists' hands, the latter may succeed in winning popular support. Alternatively, terrorists may seek to create divisions within the community, or to intensify those that already exist. Some Islamic extremists seek to provoke wide-scale conflict between believers and infidels.

Conclusion

Despite their differences, organized crime and terrorism have much in common. Both have proven to be formidable challenges for democratic societies in the new millennium. The chapters that follow will further explore these themes, and suggest policies through which the two types of illicit activity can be managed without further compromising the democratic principles that they threaten.

TWO
dimensions of the problem

Introduction

This chapter summarizes descriptive information on terrorism and organized crime. First it will discuss the quality of data available from various official sources on both types of illegality, and will review recent trends. Second, it will identify forms of terror, and distinguish between cyber crime and cyber terror. Third, it will examine the crucial role of the financing of terror and the overlap of terrorism with conventional crime and criminals. Finally, it will explore domestic and transnational crime as threats to national and regional security.

Terrorism and organized crime: How much is there? Where is it heading?

It would be nice to have a clear picture of the magnitude and scope of organized crime and terrorism – comprehensive data that would enable rigorous comparison over time and across jurisdictions. However, given the definitional and conceptual problems discussed in Chapter 1, complete statistics on organized crime and terrorism remain an elusive goal.

As we have seen, sovereign states enact their own criminal legislation, specifying what acts are criminal and differentiating them from those acts that are legal. These specifications often focus on the act, rather than the motive or social circumstances of the perpetrator. An armed robbery is an armed robbery, whether it is the work of a gang of professional robbers, a lone individual, or terrorists seeking to finance a forthcoming operation.

For a variety of reasons, many acts of crime – and even of terrorism – never reach official attention. When a crime involves the provision of illicit goods and services, there may not be a tangible, proximate victim. In the case of some crimes, such as extortion, the victim may be silenced by the actual or perceived threat of retaliation. Many retail merchants pay off their 'protectors' and suffer in silence. Some crimes are so skillfully executed that even the victim is unaware of the situation: charitable contribution fraud can leave the victim with a warm feeling of well-being rather than a sense of being defrauded. Inchoate offences such as conspiracy may never be detected, especially if the ultimate crime is abandoned before it is executed.

But what of those crimes that are completed by the offender(s), reported by the victim(s), and recorded by the authorities? In some cases, the organizational circumstances of the perpetrator may not be apparent. Sophisticated investigation may be able to attribute a particular incident of motor vehicle theft to a specific criminal organization, but not all investigators are omniscient. Lee Harvey Oswald, the assassin of John F. Kennedy, was himself killed soon after by Jack Ruby. Conventional wisdom, and the findings of a Presidential Commission, held that Oswald and Ruby each acted alone. But a great deal of circumstantial evidence suggests that both may have been involved with various criminal associates (Kaiser, 2008).

Many acts of organized crime are violations of conventional criminal law and are thus 'counted' as ordinary offences. The context or the ends of the crime in question may be unapparent or disregarded.

As responsibility for different types of crime may be shared within and between governmental jurisdictions, there may be no comprehensive centralized statistical collection. Divisions of labor and statistical habits of various law enforcement agencies may mean that information is not recorded consistently. An agency's capacity to identify and to enumerate illegal activity often depends on the resources at its disposal. Investing more resources in customs inspection, all else being equal, will lead to identification of more smuggled contraband. A specialized youth gang division may perceive more youth crime as gang related.

Some small jurisdictions lack the administrative infrastructure to collect crime statistics of any significant value.

The scale of organized crime can also defy quantification. Consider a group of criminals who use botnets (robot computer networks) to send an advance free fraud letter to a million prospective victims. If one applies the accounting principle 'one victim, one offence,' that adds up to a million offences. Other accounting systems may record this as one offence, committed by multiple offenders. The 9/11 attacks involved 19 offenders, four aircraft, and thousands of victims. Was this one incident, or four, or thousands?

The sheer diversity of organized crime also inhibits comprehensive quantification. Extortion, piracy (both on the high seas and in cyber-space), people smuggling, the manufacture and distribution of illicit drugs, and numerous other offences may occur across borders or in international waters. Statistics on terrorism are usually produced by agencies of government, who often have a stake in the perceived need for their services, or in the public's perception of the quality of their service delivery. There are thus many institutional actors with vested interests in amplifying or in muting the magnitude of terrorist or organized criminal activity. They may also reflect certain national priorities. The US Department of State, for example, is less attentive to terrorist activity seen as not impacting on US interests than to those acts of terrorism which do.

What we have then is a 'dog's breakfast' of selective measurements, which significantly inhibit our ability to generalize across time and space. It is not possible to say that globally (or often even within one's own country), there was more organized criminal activity last year than there is this year. What we do have is a mosaic, comprised of a few clear images, others quite blurred, and some missing altogether.[4]

---

[4]A great deal also depends on the analytic incision that is made into the phenomenon: Cressey (1969) relied on FBI wire taps and the McClellan Commission, which disclosed a picture of a bureaucratic monolith; Ianni and Reuss Ianni (1972) on a social anthropology which revealed kinship patterns; Teresa and Valachi on reminiscence which was about the exercise of power in a proto-feudal group (Maas, 1968); Bell on market provision and functional adjustment to dilemmas of power; Gambetta (1996) on rational choice and exchange; Blok (1975) on a power vacuum; and Hobbs (2001) on observations that led him to register contingency, pragmatics and flux. One sees what one's ideas permit one to see.

Maritime piracy is certainly an organized crime, usually an offence against the law of the country in whose territorial waters the act occurs, if not the country where the ship is registered. The International Maritime Organization publishes monthly reports of all acts of piracy and armed robbery of ships coming to its attention. (http://www.imo.org/Circulars/index.asp?topic_id=334). Given the nature of piracy we can say with some degree of confidence that it has increased significantly since 2006 (see Table 2.1), especially in the waters off the Horn of Africa. But we also know that the greater attention now being focused on the crime of piracy will also likely contribute to an increase in the reporting of the crime, a phenomenon that is quite common in the compilation of crime statistics.

Table 2.1   Reports of Maritime Piracy 2004–2009

2009	406
2008	293
2007	263
2006	239
2005	276
2004	329

Source: ICC Commercial Crime Services, 2010
http://www.imo.org/Circulars/index.asp?topic_id=334
(accessed 6 July 2010)

The United Nations Office of Drugs and Crime (UNODC) publishes an annual World Drug Report containing estimates and trends in production, trafficking and consumption in various illicit drug markets, including opium/heroin, coca/cocaine, cannabis and amphetamine-type stimulants. Appended to the Report is a statistical section that contains information for selected countries and drug types with regards to drug seizures, seizures of illicit laboratories, wholesale and retail (street) prices, and per capita consumption data.

In addition, the UNODC has an online database that allows users to access annual totals of seizures for a range of illicit drug types by year for individual countries around the world (http://www.unodc.org/unodc/en/data-and-analysis/Research-Database.html). The data are collected by means of a questionnaire administered annually to member nations. Unfortunately, many of them fail to provide the data requested.

The US Drug Enforcement Administration (DEA), with an annual budget in excess of US$2.3 billion, can afford to publish comprehensive statistics on its activities. But even the DEA does not differentiate in terms of the organizational context in which seizures occur. A look at Table 2.2 will show that the most significant trend in the past 20 years has been an increase in seizures of amphetamines. One also notes several large LSD seizures in the year 2000. It seems likely that the production of synthetic illicit drugs has increased since the turn of the century. But of course, it is difficult to know from the data if law enforcement has improved or if the seizures are simply a constant percentage of the illicit drugs produced.

The European Union has a law enforcement office (EUROPOL) whose primary responsibility is criminal intelligence, with particular regard for organized crime. EUROPOL, with headquarters in The Hague, publishes annual threat assessments, which are narrative rather than quantitative (see EUROPOL, 2008). In addition, it provides advice and assistance to EU member states.

Some countries produce regular narrative and or statistical reports on crime generally, which may include sections devoted to organized crime. For example, the Japanese government's annual White Paper on Crime contains a special section on trends in offences related to *boryokudan* (*yakuza* or organized crime groups) and their members (Ministry of Justice, Japan, 2008). From this, we learn that the number of regular members of criminal organizations declined by 6 percent from 1996–2005, but the number of 'quasi members' increased by 26 percent over the same period. Few if any other countries are able to enumerate their population of organized criminals with such precision, given that realities of organizational life make for both greater fluidity in organizational membership and greater secrecy on the part of illicit organizations and their members.

In the UK, a special organization was created at the national level in 2006 to address organized crime. Called the Serious Organized Crime Agency (SOCA), it produces a UK National Threat Assessment, but this, like the document published by EUROPOL, is more qualitative than statistical. So too are the annual reports on organized crime published by the Criminal Intelligence Service of Canada (CISC) (2008). Neither qualitative nor quantitative data provide perfect knowledge of organized

Table 2.2 Drug Seizures by US Drug Enforcement Administration

DEA Drug Seizures

Calendar Year	Cocaine kgs	Heroin kgs	Marijuana kgs	Methamphetamine kgs	Hallucinogens dosage units
2009	49,339	642	666,120	1,703	2,954,251
2008	49,823.3	598.6	660,969.2	1,540.4	9,199,693
2007	96,713	625	356,472	1,086	5,636,305
2006	69,826	805	322,438	1,711	4,606,277
2005	118,311	640	283,344	2,161	8,881,321
2004	117,854	672	265,813	1,659	2,261,706
2003	73,725	795	254,196	1,678	2,878,594
2002	63,640	710	238,024	1,353	11,661,157
2001	59,430	753	271,849	1,634	13,755,390
2000	58,674	546	331,964	1,771	29,307,427
1999	36,165	351	338,247	1,489	1,736,077
1998	34,447	370	262,180	1,203	1,075,457
1997	28,670	399	215,348	1147	1,100,912
1996	44,735	320	192,059	751	1,719,209
1995	45,326	876	219,830	876	2,768,165
1994	75,051	491	157,181	768	1,366,817
1993	55,529	616	143,055	560	2,710,063
1992	69,324	722	201,483	352	1,305,177
1991	67,016	1,174	98,592	289	1,297,394
1990	57,031	535	127,792	272	2,826,966
1989	73,587	758	286,371	896	13,125,010
1988	60,951	728	347,306	694	16,706,442
1987	49,666	512	629,839	198	6,556,891
1986	29,389	421	491,831	234.5	4,146,329

Source: DEA (STRIDE)

CY 2000 had several large LSD Seizures

Administration http://www.usdoj.gov/dea/statistics.html – stories

http://www.justice.gov/dea/statistics.html#seizures (accessed 10 August 2010) crime or terrorism. But they do provide complementary information that enhances our understanding of patterns and trends.

The adaptability of organized criminals

The most resourceful organized criminals will seek out new opportunities when they present themselves, and abandon old practices when they are no longer profitable or become dangerous. With the rapid economic development of greater China, the popularity of the shellfish abalone increased dramatically, and so did its price. Abalone fisheries in Australia became prime targets for poachers. Favorable growing conditions in British Columbia and the proximity of an insatiable market for cannabis across the US border led to cannabis becoming one of the province's major exports, responsible for five percent of its GDP. In the United States, aggressive border controls to interdict heroin and cocaine have made it more attractive for some entrepreneurs to manufacture synthetic illicit drugs such as methamphetamine. Once again, crime follows opportunity.

The complexity and sophistication of some contemporary crime may require critical skills for their execution. For example, the large scale manufacture of synthetic illicit drugs may depend upon the services of a professional chemist. Securities fraud and money laundering may be more easily accomplished in collaboration with financial professionals. These and other strategically situated actors may be referred to as 'crime facilitators' (Levi et al., 2005). To this end, conventional organized criminals may seek to recruit such specialized expertise through inducement or coercion.

Trends in organized crime

While some forms of organized crime (such as routine extortion) have changed little over the years, other aspects have changed significantly. Ethnically based hierarchies on the traditional Mafia model have been eclipsed by temporary, opportunistic coalitions of relatively small groups. Rather than 'do-it-yourself' activity, specialized services, from financial engineering to chemistry, are engaged on a project-by-project basis.

In substantive terms, four types of crime have become increasingly prevalent in the new millennium, or at least have attracted the interest of authorities in western democracies. We have already mentioned maritime piracy. The use of digital technology as an instrument and as a target of organized crime also ranks high on this list. As an increasing amount of commercial activity occurs in cyberspace, it is not surprising that it has attracted the attention of organized criminals. Organized theft of personal identification information, and specifically credit card details, is perhaps the most prominent.

The manufacture of synthetic illicit drugs, most notably amphetamine type substances and so-called party drugs like ecstasy, have eclipsed opioids, hallucinogens and cocaine to rival cannabis as the most popular recreational drugs over the past decade. The UN Office of Drugs and Crime estimates that worldwide, between 16–51 million people between the ages of 15 and 64 used amphetamine-type substances at least once in 2007 (UNODC, 2009: 15). Authorities in English speaking democracies have identified 'outlaw motorcycle gangs' as among the more prominent of those involved in the manufacture of synthetic party drugs.

The fourth visible trend is trafficking and smuggling in human beings. The rapid increase in population movement that has been facilitated by technology, combined with the lure of affluence and political stability in the developed world, have made it tempting and profitable to assist individuals in circumventing the traditional legal requirements of immigration. Whether the individuals in question are fleeing real political persecution, or whether they are economic opportunists merely seeking a better life for themselves, they may need to rely on illicit services to reach their destinations. In so doing they may be vulnerable to extortion or to brutal exploitation. Some of the worst cases are tantamount to slavery. An indication of the increased volume of displaced persons during the first decade of the present century may be found in Table 2.3.

Table 2.3 Internationally displaced persons protected/assisted by UN High Commissioner for Refugees, 2000–2008

2000	5,998,501
2001	5,096,502
2002	4,646,641
2003	4,181,701
2004	5,426,539
2005	6,616,791
2006	12,794,268
2007	13,594,009
2008	14,354,219

Source: UNHCR
http://www.unhcr.org

Forms of terror

The most common manifestations of contemporary terrorism are bombings, kidnappings and assassinations.

Explosive devices can be positioned, and then detonated when disturbed by the victim. They can be set off by a timing device. Or, they may be detonated by remote control using devices as simple as a mobile phone. Alternatively, they may be ignited directly by the bearer, as is the case with suicide bombers. Perhaps the most dramatic example is that of the 9/11 attacks, where aircraft were hijacked, and then used as flying bombs against prominent or heavily populated targets. Other potential instruments of terror, which certainly pose risks but which have yet to be employed on a significant scale, include chemical, biological, or radiological weapons. In addition, the term 'cyber-terrorism' has been used to refer to the use of the internet and related technology as instruments or as targets of a terror attack.

Targeted assassinations have been a common tactic of terrorist groups for centuries. The most common victims are senior public officials, although persons of relatively junior status such as police officers and military personnel are often targeted.

The related tactic of kidnapping is also common, in locations as diverse as Colombia, Pakistan, and the Philippines. Kidnapping may be done for ransom, in order to support other terrorist operations, to acquire hostages for use in extracting concessions from an adversary, or they may be done for psychological effect. Images of beheadings of kidnap victims may be disseminated around the globe on the internet.

Terrorism takes many forms. It can be the work of a lone individual, a small circle of associates, an organized group, or the state itself. Motives of terrorists can vary from generalized protest, to revenge in response to a perceived injustice, to regime change or, perhaps, to affirm a sense of manhood in a disempowering world. It appears that a number of terrorist movements, and many individual acts of terrorism, are driven by resentment over the presence of foreign forces in one's homeland. Osama bin Laden, for one, has expressed outrage at the presence of US forces in Saudi Arabia, the birthplace of Islam.

The Unabomber, who sent carefully prepared package bombs through the post to selected individuals in the United States between 1978 and 1995, acted very much alone. The Unabomber, a reclusive mathematician named Theodore Kaczynski, was protesting at what he saw as the loss of human freedom arising from modern organizations and technology. Timothy McVeigh, the Oklahoma City bomber, sought revenge against what he saw as a tyrannical federal government. He was particularly incensed by the Waco siege of 1993, where 76 members of a religious sect died after a standoff with US authorities.

State terrorism

State terrorism too, is very diverse. When states engage in terrorism, they may seek to repress their own citizens, or to achieve some political objective vis-à-vis another state or some non-state group. State complicity in terrorism can vary, from the actual conduct of terrorist activity by state employees, acts undertaken by private contractors, acts of private citizens that are facilitated or encouraged by the state, and acts that are condoned by the state, or where the state turns a blind eye to terrorist acts that serve its interests.

Cyber crime and cyber-terrorism

When a government or major commercial website is attacked, it may not be readily apparent whether the perpetrator is a fifteen year old operating from his bedroom; an organized crime group; or agents of a foreign government. Recall the definition of terrorism provided in Chapter 1: 'an act or threat of violence to create fear and/or compliant conduct in a victim or wider audience for the purpose of achieving political ends.' In addition, it may not be entirely clear whether the perpetrator is merely being mischievous, inquisitive, boastful, preparing for a more serious attack, or intending to intimidate the target government and its citizenry.

What then, is cyber-terrorism? Professor Dorothy Denning (2000) defines cyber-terrorism as 'unlawful attacks against computers, networks and the information stored therein when done to intimidate or coerce a government or its people in furtherance of political or social objectives.' This is what some people in the United States refer to as the 'Electronic Pearl Harbor' scenario. Others use the expression 'Electronic Armageddon.' But the terms *intimidate, coerce* and *political* remain crucial.

It is important to keep in mind that a great deal of cybercrime is committed by lone individuals for fun, for the intellectual challenge, and for protest and rebellion rather than for purposes of coercion or intimidation. As such, these acts constitute neither terrorism nor organized crime. The vast majority of those website defacements, denial of service attacks, viruses, and attacks on critical infrastructure that have occurred in the two decades since the dawn of the digital age, cannot be regarded as terrorism. Having said that, critical infrastructure such as power generation, water supply, air traffic control, communications, financial systems, and electronic commerce are all vulnerable to electronic disruption and could all be targeted in a terrorist attack. The cyber attacks against government servers in Estonia in April, 2007 apparently sought to intimidate the Estonian government and its people for having relocated a Soviet-era memorial to fallen Russian soldiers. Russia's invasion of Georgia in August 2008 was also accompanied by cyber attacks against Georgian government sites. In both cases the degree to which the Russian government was complicit in the attacks was unclear. But neither case rises to the level of terrorism.

Although actual examples of cyber-terrorism may be rare, there are many ways in which terrestrial terrorists do use digital technology in furtherance of their activities. Some terrorists engage in cybercrime in order to acquire resources with which to finance terrorist operations. Imam Samudra, convicted architect of the 2002 Bali bombings, reportedly called upon his followers to commit credit card fraud (Sipress, 2004).

Digital technology enables access to open source intelligence and to classified information, if one succeeds in hacking into an adversary's computer systems. Aerial photographs of most parts of the globe are readily available on the World Wide Web. Digital technology facilitates communications among terrorists, just as it does among honest, law abiding people. Technologies of *encryption* (scrambling the content of a message) and *steganography* (concealing a message within a digital image) make the content more difficult for investigators to access. And of course, the internet lends itself perfectly to communicating across widely dispersed elements of a network.

The internet greatly facilitates the dissemination of propaganda, and does not require access to conventional media organizations and editorial processes. Images depicting the abuse of prisoners at Abu Ghraib, or successful terrorist operations, can circulate freely in cyberspace in a manner calculated to rally support for the terrorist cause. In addition, terrorists and their supporters may use it for purposes of tactical deception, by creating the illusion of enhanced online activity. This is called 'chatter.'

They can also use it to publicize hostage takings and hostages' pleas for mercy, not to mention actual executions. Communicating an act or threat of violence to coerce or intimidate a wider audience for political ends is real terrorism.

Terrorists can also use the internet for fundraising and recruitment. Jihadist websites and chat rooms abound in cyberspace. And digital technology can also be harnessed for the training of terrorists. The information once contained in bulky training manuals can now be easily stored on a flash drive, concealed through encryption, and posted on a password-protected website.

Measuring terrorism

There have been numerous attempts to systematize data on terrorism but the collection and presentation of public data has been fraught with difficulties. In addition to the problems inherent in any cross-national data collection process there are a number of issues that are particularly problematic in the development of reliable and comprehensive terrorism data sets.

One of the most interesting problems in the collection of terrorism events data arises from the fact that terrorism is generally distinguished from violent behaviors by the identification of the intent to create fear or compliant behavior. However, in many cases there is no information available at the time of collection about the intentions of the perpetrators and thus most often researchers must infer motivation when they construct data sets. Thus, in the collection of terrorism data, the operationalization of the concept of terrorism often does not distinguish the event from other forms of political violence because analysts ignore the implications of the bargaining/coercion/intimidation communicative foundation that we say differentiates terrorism from other kinds of violence.

In addition, data collection efforts also may not distinguish between the types of acts that are performed by persons and organizations who have been previously labeled terrorist. Thus, quite often the 'criminal' activities of terrorist organizations are considered as terrorist acts in themselves. This occurs when designated terrorist groups are involved in a bank robbery or a money laundering scheme, or smuggling. The act, because it is performed by the designated terrorist organization, is deemed an act of terrorism. This raises the important data collection question: do terrorist acts include all acts conducted by members of organizations who have conducted terrorist actions in the past? This data collection question becomes extraordinarily important when we attempt to construct explanations of who becomes a terrorist and use such data to analyze the psychological, sociological or political traits associated with terrorism. Should we include or exclude these events, and these persons, in the analysis? What impact do these choices have on our sample of events, persons, organizations and how does that influence what we think we know about terrorists and terrorism?

One must also recognize that there are only a few data bases for the study of terrorism and that the primary data bases that have been exploited thus far by scholars are composed of only a small percentage of the sum total of terrorist events. Transnational or international terrorism (terrorism which extends across national boundaries or targets 'foreign' nationals) is relatively infrequent compared to domestic terrorism (terrorism that targets the same country's nationals within the state's borders) but there are very few accessible domestic terrorism data bases and no comprehensive cross-national domestic terrorism data base. Compiling these data bases is extraordinarily time consuming, difficult and expensive and thus only a few long term efforts have been attempted. Furthermore, the majority of area or country experts who study political violence and terrorism are not inclined to create data bases (see Ross, 2004).

Databases

What data do we have and what can they tell us about terrorism? Until recently, the three most frequently used data sources on terrorism have been:

- the US government's data on International Terrorism, compiled and published from 1973–1981 by the Central Intelligence Agency, from 1982–2003 by the US Department of State and since 2004 by the National Counter Terrorism Center (NCTC);
- the Rand/St. Andrews MIPT data set; and
- ITERATE.

The Rand/St. Andrews MIPT data set has now become part of the fourth major data set:

- The Global Terrorism Data Base at the START Center at the University of Maryland.

For many years, although they focused narrowly on 'international' terrorism, the CIA and the State Department were very consistent in their methodology. While there were concerns about some incidents that were either included in or excluded from the data series, over the first 30 years in which they presented the data, until the publication of the 2003 report in April 2004 there was reasonable confidence, if one understood the parameters of the collection decisions, in the integrity of the data. This changed in 2004 when the Bush administration appeared to politicize the data and the Department of State published a very flawed report (see

Krueger and Laitin, 2004). The flaws in that report highlighted the very clear manner in which political decisions might easily influence the compilation of the data set, but there are other issues as well that create problems for our confidence that these data provide a 'complete' picture of the dimensions of the terrorism problem.[5] Box 2.1 describes how each source has described itself.

Box 2.1   Terrorism Data Bases

RAND Terrorism Chronology 1968–1997 and RAND®-MIPT Terrorism Incident database (1998–Present)

'The RAND Terrorism Chronology 1968–1997 serves to monitor all international terrorism incidents and to make them available to the public. All information was taken from open source materials, such as newspapers and every effort was made to verify the accuracy of the information found in the reports. This database is intended only to aid those seeking to better comprehend terrorism and should not be used as a tool for any sort of analysis, predictive or otherwise.'

'The RAND®-MIPT Terrorism Incident database (1998–Present) serves to monitor all terrorism incidents worldwide, both domestic and international, and to make them available to the public. All information was taken from open source materials, such as newspapers and every effort was made to verify the accuracy of the information found in the reports. **This database is intended only to aid those seeking to better comprehend terrorism and should not be used as a tool for any sort of analysis, predictive or otherwise'** (emphasis added). http://www.tkb.org/RandSummary.jsp

---

[5]Krueger and Laitin argued that in 2004 the preparers of the data set, for the first time, not only presented results for less than a calendar year (ending the analysis on November 11 rather than December 31), but also did not report that they had done so. One important consequence was that the number of reported attacks and casualties dropped for the year reported. In addition, the analysts also appeared to have altered the operational definition of significant events so that the number of non-significant events increased while significant events dropped. This clear violation of basic social science rules of measurement was compounded by 'rampant' arithmetic errors in the report. All of these charges were later acknowledged by the agencies involved. What remains at issue was whether these errors were the result of political manipulation.

> ITERATE 'has relied on press, television and radio reports – mainly through the mainstream media, and including US and foreign outlets – international news services, accounts in scholarly journals, books, memoirs, interviews with principals, and so on … although the State Department, ITERATE, and Rand corporation compilations have roughly similar inclusion and coding conventions, differences nonetheless remain that could befoul any attempts at dataset mergers (Mickolus, 2002: 153).

These are the two most widely used non-governmental data sets for the analysis of terrorism. The RAND/MIPT actually cautions us not to use the data for analysis. The first thing one should notice beyond that is ITERATE, throughout its history, has focused on international terrorism events. The RAND data set focused on international events until 1997 and then shifted to include both domestic and international events in 1998 and later years.

In the past few years a new data set has become available, the Global Terrorism Database (GTD) at the START program at the University of Maryland. They describe the data set as 'an open-source database including information on terrorist events around the world from 1970 through 2007 (with annual updates planned for the future). Unlike many other event databases, the GTD includes systematic data on domestic as well as transnational and international terrorist incidents that have occurred during this time period and now includes more than 80,000 cases. For each GTD incident, information is available on the date and location of the incident, the weapons used and nature of the target, the number of casualties, and – when identifiable – the group or individual responsible.

Somewhat troubling is the following explanation appearing within a frequently asked questions section about the data base:

…While the GTD inclusion criteria offer a comprehensive definition of terrorism, we encourage users to take advantage of the GTD's flexibility to restrict the data according to their definitional preferences. This includes filtering search results based on whether the coder noted some uncertainty whether an incident meets all of the criteria for inclusion. ('Doubt Terrorism Proper,' available for post-1997 cases only)

Thus, without a detailed analysis of the data one cannot determine how many of the 80,000 events actually meet the operational definition.

There are a number of important potential limitations that anyone using these data sets must consider. First, the major data sets are all heavily dependent upon media reports for their compilation. This has certain important consequences. Media coverage of the world at large, despite the globalization of communication, is still very uneven. Western Europe, North America and the richer parts of Asia, Latin America and Oceania are more likely to receive coverage than Africa and the poorer parts of Asia, Latin America and Oceania unless rich countries are fighting wars (especially wars of interest to the developed world) in those regions. Killing an American or a Western European is more likely to generate the international coverage upon which the data sets depend than killing a non-westerner, independent of the geographic location.

Secondly, each of these data bases is far more concerned with insurgent international terrorism than domestic terrorism or state terrorism. Further, there is clear evidence that the violence of state terrorism and domestic terrorism has been consistently more deadly than international terrorism, and thus our main sources of data that have been the subject of analysis over the past 40 years actually cover the smallest part of the potential terrorism data set (see Stohl, 2006; Rummel, 1997). Nonetheless, there are some very interesting and useful pieces of information that we can glean from the existing data sets, which despite their differences reveal rather consistent overall patterns.

Before looking at the data it is important to realize that generally when we begin to consider the problem of international terrorism it is the 'terrorist spectacular' such as 9/11 or the 7/7 London bombings (2005) or the bombing of the Madrid Atocha Train Station[6] that immediately come to the minds of most observers. These incidents are deadly, significant and luckily not typical representations of terrorist

---

[6]On 11 March, 2004, commuter trains in Madrid were subjected to a coordinated bombing attack. The operation, which resulted in 191 dead and 1,841 injured, were found to have been the work of an Al Qaeda inspired terrorist group (BBC News, 2007).

events. As we indicated earlier, it is still likely that as Brian Jenkins observed (1975: 15), terrorists want a lot of people watching, not a lot of people dead. The data continue to bear this out.

Recognizing that we are examining only international events, analysis of the data sets discussed above indicates that the frequency of international terrorist incidents has been characterized by a series of peaks and valleys over the last three decades. After climbing to over 300 events per year in the early 1970s, the number of terrorist events varied between 290 and a high of almost 600 (578) events in 1991, before dropping dramatically to a low of 95 in 1998. Spiking upwards to 295 in 1999 it again dropped to a new 30 year low before the events of 9/11. Currently, the number of events is again rising but, if one is careful about how one characterizes the violent events within Iraq during the period after the start of the Iraq War, or in Afghanistan following the start of that war, the number of events does not rise again to the mean or median levels of the 1968–1999 period.

According to the ITERATE data, about 11,650 international terrorist incidents occurred between 1968 and 2001. Eighty-five and one half percent of the global acts of terrorism did not result in fatalities. Another 8 percent were characterized by a single death. In total, fatality-free and single-death incidents accounted for 93.6 percent of all global terrorist incidents. The total number of recorded deaths from incidents of global terrorism for the 30 years before 11 September was just over 10,000. In those 30 years there were approximately twice as many people wounded as killed.

In the vast majority of international terrorist incidents (over 82 percent) nobody was wounded, and in another 685 (6.3 percent) only one person was wounded per incident. In almost 90 percent of these recorded terrorist events, one or no persons were even injured. Although big events with many deaths and injuries are in our consciousness, none or few deaths and injury-free events are the 'reality' for most incidents of international terrorism. Furthermore, according to the ITERATE data, most incidents of international terrorism produce no property damage at all. As Enders and Sandler (2005: 259) write 'Perhaps surprisingly little has changed in the time series of overall incidents and most of its component series.'

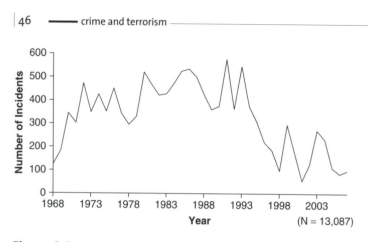

Figure 2.1 International terrorist incidents 1968–2007
Figure prepared by Peter Flemming based on ITERATE data.

Trends in terrorism

The events of September 11, 2001 and the Omagh bombing of 1998 brought home the abhorrent reality of terrorism to much of the world's population. They even altered the political calculus of some oppositional groups, even as the event was applauded in some quarters. Groups like the IRA, realizing that armed struggle was no longer likely to win hearts and minds, soon embraced a political settlement. Activities of the Basque separatist group ETA also became more moderate, at least in the short term. On the other hand, for people who considered the United States the enemy, or at least the supporter of their enemy, the September 11 attacks were evidence that even the most powerful nation could be hurt and made to feel the pain that they considered to be inflicted regularly upon themselves.

But the lingering wars in Iraq and Afghanistan have both been accompanied by persistent terrorist activity, directed not only against occupying forces, but also against civilian populations and their governments.

One form of terrorism that has increased in recent years is suicide terrorism. Although not a uniquely modern phenomenon (Pape 2005; Gambetta 2005), suicide terrorism has become a weapon of choice in some parts of the world.

Another trend in terrorism is reflected in the transformation of Al Qaeda from an *organization* into something more of a *movement*. The intense pursuit of Al Qaeda by the US and its allies in the aftermath of 9/11 almost certainly succeeded in neutralizing a number of significant members and in significantly weakening the ability of the central leadership to organize and communicate with its members, thus weakening its capacity to plan and execute further terrorist 'spectaculars.' However, some aspects of the so-called 'war on terror,' particularly the perceived heavy-handedness in the confinement and interrogation of terrorist suspects, generated widespread moral indignation and in some quarters, sympathy for the terrorist cause. With militant ideology and examples of terrorist activity widely accessible over the internet, it appears that some groups acted in the manner of independent franchisees, fulfilling the spirit of Al Qaeda without actually taking direct orders. It might even be possible to argue that, for certain purposes, Al Qaeda is functionally acephalous.

Financing terror

Compared to the billions of dollars spent by governments and private industry in the global war on terrorism, terrorists themselves come cheap. It was estimated that the total cost of the coordinated attacks of September 11, 2001 was approximately USD$500,000. The Oklahoma City bombing required little more than the rental of a truck and the purchase of an appropriate quantity of fertilizer and fuel oil. An individual suicide bomber can be outfitted very inexpensively. Although the bombers' relatives may receive some financial consideration after the fact, the amount is usually modest.

However modest, and even if carried out by volunteer labor, terrorist operations do require a degree of finance. Osama bin Laden, a man of considerable wealth, was able to spend some his wealth in support of his operations. However, he and most groups require substantial additional funds to maintain their organizations. The IRA, for example, was heavily dependent not only on criminal activities but also upon fund-raising operations carried out in the United States through 'charitable fronts.' In the aftermath of September 11, Western governments have closed down a number of Islamic charities which, they alleged, provided funds to terrorist groups.

Terrorists also resort to conventional criminality to finance their operations. Ransom kidnapping has been a very lucrative practice, particularly in places like Colombia. Ransom kidnapping was also practiced by European terrorist groups in the 1970s and 1980s. Kidnapping was also committed to reinforce demands for the release of imprisoned terrorists. The most prominent victim of such an offence was former Italian Prime Minister Aldo Moro, who was killed by the Red Brigades when their demands were not met.

More recently, it is alleged that the Tamil Tigers engaged in credit card and ATM fraud for revenue-raising. We have already noted the encouragement of cyber crime by militants in Indonesia.

Government efforts to interdict terrorist financing, or to trace the source of such funds, has been based on the cash transactions reporting framework originally established in response to organized crime and tax evasion. Particular concern has been voiced about the use of informal payment systems, called *hawala*, for remittances across national borders outside of the formal financial system. One of the most challenging aspects of counterterrorism is to ensure that interventions are targeted carefully and do not have an adverse impact on innocent third parties. The interdiction of informal transfer payments may significantly impede the flow of remittances from expatriate guest workers to their families in the world's poorer nations (Passas, 2006).

Terrorist financing methods include the following:

- so called 'revolutionary taxes' (extortion) are most important for large cadre based organizations such as the Maoists (India), New People's Army (NPA) (Philippines), FARC (Colombia)

- sale of pornographic material (North-east of India)

- narco-terrorism (Colombia, Burma, Afghanistan, etc.)

- ransom kidnapping (Colombia – FARC), Philippines (Abu Sayyaf), India (violent jihadists)

- misuse of charities (Saudi Arabia), Philippines, Indonesia and the West generally – also used as a means of money laundering

- intellectual property piracy (tri-border area of South America)

- robbery, car re-birthing, general crime (including car re-birthing in Australia; robbery to finance the Bali bombings)

- state sponsorship (Pakistan)

- people trafficking (Pakistan)

- legitimate businesses (Al Qaeda, LTTE)

A portion of proceeds from weapons sales to Iran in 1986 on behalf of the United States were diverted and used to support insurgents in Nicaragua.

Domestic and transnational crime as a threat to national and regional security

Although one might think of national security in terms of protecting one's country against invasion or attack from abroad, crime itself can erode national security. This can occur when crime has an adverse impact on a nation's economy, public health, social cohesion, and the legitimacy of its leaders. The conceptualization of crime as a national security threat first became prominent when it featured in a speech by President Clinton to the 50th Anniversary of the UN General Assembly in 1995. Since that time, the wider implications of crime have become increasingly apparent. The message was reinforced in a national security statement published by the Australian Government in 2008 (http://www.pm.gov.au/node/5424).

Widespread drug use can impact adversely on public health and economic productivity. Taxpayers' money spent on police and prisons might otherwise be devoted to health, education, welfare, and even national defense. Corruption, which often accompanies domestic or transnational crime, can lead to a loss of legitimacy of police and/or government, and an ultimate weakening of a state. Laundering money through a small nation's economy can impact on exchange rates, diminish tax revenues, and reduce the competitiveness of traditional exports.

Many crimes have international repercussions. In the late 1990s, a massive fraud resulted in a significant number of Albanians losing their life savings. This was followed by the collapse of the Albanian government, and a substantial exodus of Albanians seeking refuge in neighboring Italy, with consequent strains on Italian law enforcement, emergency services, and immigration resources. State terrorism too can produce flows of refugees that can place great burdens on potential host states. In some countries, crime poses so much of a risk that foreign investment and tourism are not economically feasible.

National security is not an either/or phenomenon. The security of a given state at a given time can be located on a continuum between impregnability on the one hand, and collapse on the other. Various factors, of which crime is but one, will determine a state's location on that continuum, and its movement in one direction or another.

Some states are so weakened by crime, corruption and other factors that they become 'criminal havens' where criminals can operate with impunity. This poses problems for healthier states, since criminal havens can serve as trans-shipment points or places of refuge for transnational offenders. Criminal havens can also be terrorist havens. Contemporary Somalia, with its mix of pirates and militant Islamists is but one example. It is not coincidental that much maritime piracy is based in Somalia, which has been without effective government since 1991.[7]

The 'flip side' of counterterrorist policing is its effect on conventional crime. This can occur on both strategic and operational dimensions. Preoccupation with actual or perceived terrorist threats may come at the expense of attention to grass roots problem-solving and building community relationships. Moreover, personnel who might otherwise be engaged in the investigation of conventional crime may be diverted to counterterrorism operations. On the other hand, the considerable strengthening of borders and improvement in intelligence sharing triggered by the post-9/11 concern about terrorism may also have greatly strengthened border protection vis-à-vis international crime such as drug and people smuggling.

---

[7]Ironically, some states may be strengthened by crime. Switzerland, the Cayman Islands, Luxembourg, and Lichtenstein have all benefited from their role as white collar criminal havens.

THREE

state terrorism and state crime: the dark side of the state

This chapter explores the use of crime and terror by the state. We examine how states use crime and terror as instruments of political power and the links between state actors and criminals and terrorists. We also discuss how and for what purposes states provide support for criminal and terrorist activities within their own national borders, as well as state sponsorship of transnational terrorism and criminality across borders into neighboring and distant states.

When the problems of terrorism and crime are introduced, our most common images in the contemporary mediated environment are Osama bin Laden and Tony Soprano, the Islamic terrorist and fictional mafia don. We approach terrorism and crime as activities done by insurgents and criminals against the interests of the state and its people. In this chapter, we will see that in opposition to these readily available images, terrorism and crime are hardly the monopoly of political dissidents and other non-state actors, but are rather too often the activities of government officials and agents of the state.

State terror

State terror against its own citizens

At one extreme was Soviet-era terror under Stalin, where millions were either executed, imprisoned, sent to internal exile in Siberia or deported. The objective of the Great Terror, as it came to be called, was to denounce (and to discourage) disloyalty or corruption. Similar campaigns of terror were the work of the Nazi regime (1933–45), the Idi Amin regime in Uganda, the apartheid regime in South Africa, and many others.

States can also target their citizens living abroad. The Bulgarian government was suspected of assassinating dissident Georgi Markov in London in 1978. Assassination of anti-apartheid exiles in London, Mozambique and elsewhere was South African state policy before the transition to democracy (O'Brien, 2000).

State facilitation of another state's terrorism

States may also provide assistance to another state in furtherance of the latter's terrorist activity. The US government provided law enforcement assistance to repressive Latin American regimes during the 1970s and 1980s (Huggins, 1991).

State terror against another state

In 1983, North Korean agents detonated a bomb in Burma killing 21 people, among whom were South Korean cabinet ministers on an official visit who were the target of the attack.

State terror against private interests

States may attack private individuals or NGOs. In 1985 two agents of the French government bombed the Greenpeace vessel Rainbow Warrior in the Auckland harbor, New Zealand, killing a crewmember.

In other circumstances, private interests, by their nature or location, are symbolic representatives of states. Libyan agents who engineered the Lockerbie bombing in 1988 chose an American carrier, Pan Am.

In 1986, Libyan agents bombed a nightclub in Berlin that was popular with US military personnel.

It has become commonplace in public administration to rely on private sector service providers to perform duties which in earlier times may have been performed by government employees. When states enlist the services of terrorists, either implicitly or by turning a 'blind eye' to their activities, they are often seeking what is called 'plausible deniability.' That is, by commissioning others to do the work the government may claim that they were not involved in the terrorist activity, which they characterize as the work of rogue outsiders. Proof of actual complicity may be difficult if not impossible to achieve, and governments maintain that their 'hands are clean.'

State facilitation of private actors

States may provide a safe haven to non-state actors engaged in terrorism. The Taliban regime in Afghanistan hosted Al Qaeda prior to the attacks of September 11, 2001. States may also assist terrorist groups active in other countries; Iran has supported Hezbollah in Lebanon, and the United States supported anti-Castro insurgents over the years and the Nicaraguan resistance during the 1980s.

When we begin to consider the abuse of power by the state or its criminal activities, it is also the case that we tend to think in terms of non-democratic states, i.e. dictatorships or authoritarian governments. After all, how could a government – at least a legitimate government – be thought to engage in terrorism or crime (although that thought is a little easier after the Bush administration)? This is perfectly consistent with our most common conceptions of the state and governance. For much of the past century, following Weber, social scientists have identified the state as 'that human community, which, within a given territory (territory is one of its characteristics) claims for itself (successfully) the legitimate monopoly of physical violence' (Gerth and Mills, 1958: 78). Thus by definition the state's use of violence is legitimate, and since terrorism is not legitimate, we presume legitimate states do not act as terrorists.

In short then, despite the fact that the term 'terror' first entered the French and then the English language in response to the systematic employment of violence and the guillotine by the Jacobin and

Thermidorian regimes in France, it has remained conceptually problematic to speak of state, or government, terrorism. The state is simply being itself, the repository of legitimate physical violence. However, one can define the state, as Weber does, in terms of physical violence without having to relinquish the ability to differentiate the forms in which state agencies apply that violence. That the state is defined as having the monopoly on 'legitimate violence' (if it is) does not mean that the actions of its agencies cannot be terroristic. One can define the state, as Weber does, in terms of legitimacy without having to accept all that its agents do as normatively positive. If the state, and its agency the government, have a legitimate monopoly on physical violence, it may still use that violence (and its threat) in ways as unacceptable as terrorism, mass killings and other forms of repression and human rights violations.

As we indicated in Chapter 1, while the French state under Robespierre may have been responsible for the introduction of the concept of a regime of terror, many others have followed. Iraq under the regime of Saddam Hussein (1979–2003), the Sudanese genocide (2003–), the increasingly repressive regime of Robert Mugabe in Zimbabwe, and the brutality of the Stroessner dictatorship in Paraguay (1954–1989) provide but a few examples. Like the transnational terrorism that has been the main focus of attention of scholars and statesmen, these are not 20th century phenomena that disappeared with the end of the Cold War. Indeed in the opening decade of the 21st century:

- The United Nations released a report which accused the military of Togo of killing hundreds of citizens of that country during the election campaign of 2005 and added that the military had been aided by civilian militias acting at the behest of the state;

- The United Nations Working Group on Enforced and Involuntary Disappearances (WGEID) reported that Nepal recorded the highest number of new cases of disappearances in the world, more than 1,234 cases of 'disappearance' perpetrated by security forces after May 2000 (this came in the context of a nine year brutal civil war against Maoist insurgents, who have also been responsible for grave abuses against civilians);

- In Zimbabwe, according to UN estimates, 700,000 people – nearly 6 percent of the total population – were forcibly evicted from their homes, made home-less or lost their source of livelihood beginning in May 2005 while 2.4 million people – some 18 percent of the population – were impacted by the Mugabe administration's Operation Murambatsvina;[8] and

- Human rights groups continue to report that the Turkmenistan government remains one of the most closed and brutal in the world, and continues to persecute minority religious communities such as Jehovah's Witnesses and Baptists with police raids on prayer meetings, arbitrary arrests, and beatings.

State terrorism can also occur across national frontiers. Amongst many examples are the 1976 assassination of Chilean exile Orlando Letelier in Washington DC by agents of the Chilean secret police DINA, the 1986 bombing of a German discotheque by Libyan agents targeting off-duty US military personnel, and the killings of Iranian dissidents in exile by SAVAK, the secret police of the former Shah of Iran, prior to his overthrow in 1979.

As with Weber's definition of the state being the repository of legitimate violence and therefore by implication the illegitimacy of the employment of violence by non-state actors, Abraham and van Schendel (2005: 7) argue that: 'The state's claim to a monopoly of regu-lated predation and redistribution of proceeds (i.e. taxation and state expenditure) is based on the delegitimation of other forms of predation that are constructed as robbery, piracy, fraud, warlordism, or racketeer-ing,' and thus states do not act as criminals. Paraphrasing Charles Tilly's famous phrase, 'War made the state and the state made war' (Tilly, 1975: 42), Abraham and van Schendel (2005) write '… historically the boundary of illicitness has shifted back and forth as bandits helped make states and states made bandits.' In our conception of the ideal state, the state does not engage in 'criminal' activities. However, we should note that for some (e.g. radical libertarians in the United States) all taxation by the state is theft (see the discussion in McGee, 2004: 33–40) and as Claiborne (1970: 266–267) has written, 'The distinction between robber

---

[8] Operation Murambatsvina was the name given to a program of enforced slum clearance that resulted in widespread homelessness. See International Crisis Group (2005).

and cop, between extortion and taxation, has been blurred many times in history.'[9]

Unfortunately in the contemporary world, state actors often act in criminal fashion by seizing their citizens' assets, demanding a 'cut' of profits in exchange for doing business within the country, accepting bribes or simply plundering resources within the nation. In some extreme cases it has been claimed that the state itself has become a criminal enterprise. Perl (2007) for example contends that contemporary North Korea is such a state. 'In addition to production and trafficking in heroin and methamphetamines, major sources of revenue from criminal activity for the DPRK (Democratic Republic of North Korea) now include (1) counterfeit cigarettes; (2) counterfeit pharmaceuticals (for example "USA" manufactured viagra; (3) counterfeit currency (e.g. US $100 bill "supernotes"); and (4) indiscriminate sales of small arms, i.e. "gun running." The result is a situation in which criminal activity is seen as playing an increasingly pivotal role in supporting North Korea's fragile economy.' (Perl, 2007: 15–16).

A particular form of the criminal state has led to the concept of state 'kleptocracy' (see Grossman and Noh, 1990; Bayart et al., 1999), in which the state is seen to exist to maximize the welfare of its ruler and thus is characterized by a high-level of state corruption and predation. In Liberia under Charles Taylor not only were riches in the form of money transferred from the national state to Taylor, but also the very environment was ravaged as Taylor presided over the mass deforestation of the country to obtain cash to purchase arms which were then used to maintain power and manage further exploitation. There are enough additional contemporary examples of these extreme cases, as shown in the list below, that a 'National Strategy to Fight Kleptocracy' was issued by the President of the United States in August 2006. In 2004, Transparency International released its Global Corruption Report, which highlighted the extraordinary scale of such crime identifying the ten most self-enriching leaders in recent decades. The top ten included:

1 Former Indonesian President Suharto ($15 billion–$35 billion)

2 Former Philippine President Ferdinand Marcos ($5 billion–$10 billion)

---
[9] The classic cases are those of the privateer, Vidocq, Fouché, Jonathan Wild, and others. See Rock (1977).

3 Former Zairian President Mobutu Sese Seko ($5 billion)

4 Former Nigerian President Sani Abacha ($2 billion–$5 billion)

5 Former Yugoslav President Slobodan Milošević ($1 billion)

6 Former Haitian President Jean-Claude Duvalier ($300 million–$800 million)

7 Former Peruvian President Alberto Fujimori ($600 million)

8 Former Ukrainian Prime Minister Pavlo Lazarenko ($114 million–$200 million)

9 Former Nicaraguan President Arnoldo Alemán ($100 million)

10 Former Philippine President Joseph Estrada ($78 million–$80 million)

It is important to recognize that the state's criminal capacity is not confined to its own territory. States, just as insurgent terrorists and criminals, may engage in criminal activities at home and abroad. And that is not just confined to 'illegitimate' governments. We recognize this when we argue that a current regime, acting in the name of the state, is illegitimate and rightly condemn its actions. But it is also the case that 'legitimate' regimes and governments, recognized by the international community, also may abuse their legal monopoly of force and violence, both at home and abroad, and engage in activities which could be identified as either terrorist or criminal. Indeed as Tilly argued (1985: 161), 'If protection rackets represent organized crime at its smoothest, then war making and state making – quintessential protection rackets with the advantage of legitimacy – qualify as our largest examples of organized crime.'[10]

Why state terror?

Much discussion of insurgent terrorism begins with the assertion that terrorism is a weapon of the weak. The image is of a group so unable to

---

[10] Tuchman (1978) argued that much medieval warfare was about looting rather than anything else.

engage successfully in political conflict through 'conventional' means that it adopts terrorism as a last resort out of frustration and a sense of powerlessness. Likewise, we may understand how a government may choose terror as a means of rule out of a sense of relative hopelessness in attempting to meet the (actual or perceived potential) threat through alternative means of governance. The believed relative effectiveness of terrorism in this situation depends less on the perception of terror as highly efficacious than it does on the sense that other means of rule are inefficacious and that the costs do not outweigh the benefits.

Following Gurr (1986: 62–67), one may identify three sets of conditions that affect the decision-making calculus of threatened elites: the situational, structural, and dispositional. *Situational* conditions include the political traits of challenges (the status and strategies of challengers) and the elites' own political resources for countering those challenges, i.e. the regime's strength and police and military apparatus). *Structural* conditions are those that define elites' relations with their opponents and determine or constrain their response options. These include the state's position in the international system and the nature of social stratification and the elite's position within it. *Dispositional* conditions are those which can be expected to influence how elites regard the acceptability of strategies of violence and terrorism. Norms supporting the use of violence are shaped by elites' direct or mediated experience with violent means of power and are most effectively inhibited when the society has a strongly developed history of democratic values.

Within their own societies, regimes use systematic state violence and terror as an extension of oppression or repression systems; as a method for the consolidation of power; as a reaction to 'reformist-minded' political, social, or economic organizations and their policy demands (challengers to the prevailing system); and as a reaction to an insurgent challenge to the state. The resort to terror often takes place in the context of the drive by the state for centralized control of political and economic processes (Falk, 1980), the reaction by the state to reformers and challengers (Gurr, 1986), the presence of norms and experiences to sustain terror (Gurr, 1986; Ron, 1997), and when rulers judge that there are low opportunity costs and high expectations of success (Duvall and Stohl, 1983).

A sense of the relative ineffectiveness of conventional means of rule depends on two factors: an inability of the regime to mobilize and employ the positive and negative inducements on which those means rely; and/or the non-receptivity of target groups to those inducements. A simple expectation is that the first of these factors is apt to be greatest where the regime is able to command relatively few resources and where it has relatively limited means (particularly organizational apparatus) to deliver those few resources it can command. This is most often the case in new, weak, or fragile states, particularly those which have had significant periods of violence and instability for some length of time. The non-receptivity of target groups depends overwhelmingly on the vulnerability of the group to the manipulation of positive and negative inducements by the government. Groups are less vulnerable, and hence less receptive to conventional means of governance, where they are a large proportion of the population or where they are strongly and zealously committed to the values about which they are in conflict with the regime, particularly if they are an elusive social group. Under these circumstances it is difficult for the government to buy off, co-opt, make compromises with, directly repress, or engage in physical military combat with either a large proportion of its citizenry or a deeply committed, highly zealous, generally elusive adversary group.

Also necessary are the government's expectations about the costs it would have to bear in using terrorism, relative to the costs of alternative means of governance. Two kinds of costs, response costs and production costs can be distinguished. Response costs are those costs which might be imposed by the target group and/or sympathetic or offended bystanders. The bystanders may include domestic and foreign audiences and the target audience may be wider than the attacking party may have intended when choosing the victims and the actions. Production costs are the costs of taking the action regardless of the reactions of others. In addition to the economic costs – paying the participants, buying the weapons and the like, there is the psychological cost of behaving in a manner which most individuals would, under normal conditions, characterize as unacceptable.

Thus, almost all cases of state terror are preceded by campaigns which seek to marginalize and dehumanize the potential victims and are further justified in the name of national security. When the dehumanization is 'complete,' the state has used violence to expel the 'other' from contested land (as in Bosnia) and it has used violence to exterminate the 'other' as in Rwanda, Darfur and Kosovo.

As with insurgent violence and terror, the audience to the act may be more important than the immediate victim. A government's actions may have wider purposes that the simple destruction or harm that the brute force of violence or intimidation creates. The goal includes carrying a message of intimidation and the creation of fear in the audience that the state wants to alter. Having engaged in a campaign of terrorism, the state may merely threaten in future, or simply maintain the apparatus and the official agencies of the terror to continue to terrify its population.

This is not to say that all activities of the state are conducted in the open. Campaigns of murder and intimidation have been conducted both overtly and covertly and their results both trumpeted and muted by the state, from the open genocidal policies of the Khmer Rouge to 'los desaparecidos' (the disappeared) of the authoritarian regimes of Latin America in the closing decades of the twentieth century.

States use terrorism against their own populations within and across their own state boundaries, employ their agents directly against the populations and governments of other states, or support the use of terrorism against governments and/or the populations of other states via support of other states or insurgents who are attacking the populations or governments of other states. There are two types of covert state terrorism which states employ. Clandestine state terrorism is a form of covert action which consists of direct participation by state agents in acts of terrorism. State sponsored terrorism is a form of covert action which consists of state or private groups being employed to undertake terrorist actions on behalf of the sponsoring state. It is important to understand how widespread the state's use of terror is across the globe. Stohl et al. (1984) introduced a political terror scale whose coding rules allow for the classification of five data points by which we can monitor state terror and its various manifestations. Using the yearly reports prepared by Amnesty International and the US Department of State, states are coded using the following levels on the Political Terror Scale:

1   Countries … under a secure rule of law, people are not imprisoned for their views, and torture is rare or exceptional … Political murders are extraordinarily rare.

2   There is a limited amount of imprisonment for nonviolent political activity. However, few are affected, torture and beatings are exceptional … Political murder is rare.

3   There is extensive political imprisonment, or a recent history of such imprisonment. Execution or other political murders and brutality may be common. Unlimited detention, with or without trial, for political views is accepted …

4   The practices of Level 3 are expanded to larger numbers. Murders, disappearances, and torture are a common part of life … In spite of its generality, on this level violence affects primarily those who interest themselves in politics or ideas.

5   The violence of Level 4 has been extended to the whole population … The leaders of these societies place no limits on the means or thoroughness with which they pursue personal or ideological goals.

The scale, which is produced each year, can be found at http://www. politicalterrorscale.org/about.html. In 2008 more than 30 countries had scores of 4 or higher on the scale and many had held that position by virtue of their use of violence against their citizens for more than a decade. This indicates the continued employment of state terror by substantial numbers of governments.

States have not only pursued strategies of political terror within their own boundaries to threaten their populations. Before the overthrow of the Shah of Iran in 1979, SAVAK (the Iranian National Security and Intelligence Organization) agents were known to have been employed within the United States to 'monitor' Iranian students. Colonel Qaddafi's Libyan regime was responsible for the murder of opposition figures in Rome, Athens, and London. In an infamous case noted above, the Bulgarian Secret Police, employing a poison (ricin) tipped umbrella, eliminated Georgi Markov on a London street because he criticized the Bulgarian regime in his broadcasts on the BBC. In each of these cases the regime is sending a clear message (a hallmark of political terror) to the opposition and even to the potential opposition in exile: there is no safe refuge – be afraid.

Box 3.1   State Terrorism in South Africa

During the apartheid era, the government of South Africa engaged in a range of violent activities to attack the African National Congress (ANC) and its supporters. These occurred within the borders of South Africa, elsewhere in neighbouring African nations, and as far afield as Europe. Methods employed included car, parcel and letter bombs, poison, and abductions and assassinations by armed hit squads. Torture and rape were not uncommon. Perpetrators included police, members of the South African Defence Force, mercenaries, 'hit men' and other surrogate forces.

Many ANC sympathizers were taken into custody in South Africa, only to die by 'suicide' or by 'accident.' Perhaps the most prominent of these was Stephen Biko of the Black Consciousness Movement, whose death attracted worldwide attention and widespread revulsion. Estimates of assassinations by security forces of the apartheid regime range between 50 and 110 (O'Brien, 2001).

ANC offices in at least seven countries outside South Africa were subject to sabotage attacks. In 1981 the chief representative of the ANC in Zimbabwe was shot dead in the driveway of his home in Harare. A Zimbabwean detective assigned to investigate possible South African sabotage attacks in that country was shot and killed. In 1982, the acting chief representative of the ANC in Swaziland and his wife were killed by a car bomb. Also in that year, Ruth First, the Director of the Centre for African Studies at Eduardo Mondlane University in Maputo, Mozambique was killed by a parcel bomb. In 1985 a South African undercover agent resident in Lesotho invited a number of ANC members to a Christmas party. The house was attacked and seven guests were killed. In March 1988, shortly after two unsuccessful attempts on the life of the ANC chief representative to the Benelux Countries, his counterpart in France, Ms Dulcie September, was shot to death in Paris. Also in that year, prominent ANC members in Maputo, Mozambique and Harare, Zimbabwe were seriously injured in car bomb explosions.

To further these activities the South African government established an extensive espionage network. The head of the Spanish anti-apartheid movement in the 1980s was a South African agent.

Although the outgoing government ordered the destruction of literally tons of security files, the circumstances of many of the gross human rights abuses under the Apartheid regime were disclosed by the Truth and Reconciliation Commission.

Source: South Africa, Truth and Reconciliation Commission of South Africa Report www.info.gov.za/otherdocs/2003/trc/rep.pdf (accessed 10 August 2010). O'Brien, Kevin 'Counterintelligence for counter revolutionary warfare: the South African police security branch, 1979–1990' *Intelligence and National Security*, 16 (3): 27–59.

States have also cooperated with other states across national boundaries to eliminate and terrorize their populations. McSherry (2002) details the dimensions of Operation Condor in which the repressive regimes of Latin America during the 1970s pursued the 'opposition'. Argentina, Chile, Uruguay, Paraguay, Bolivia, Brazil, and later Ecuador and Peru participated under the ideology of the National Security State (see also Pion-Berlin, 1989 and Lopez, 1986) and collaborated to allow their respective state agents to pursue, capture, terrorize and murder their citizens.

Government agents operating across national boundaries may choose either national elites or the foreign society itself as the target. In this type of state terrorism, states may thus attempt to intimidate government officials directly through campaigns of bombing, attacks, assassinations and by sponsoring and/or participating in attempted coups d'état. Alternatively, national states participate in the destabilization of other societies with the purpose of creating chaos and the conditions for the collapse of governments, the weakening of the national state and changes in leadership. The threats to the regime and the society are obvious, but there is an attempt at deniability nonetheless. Both the pattern of such behavior and the threat of such a pattern being initiated constitute the terroristic aspect of this type of action.

More than 30 years ago, Jenkins (1975) worried that states might employ groups as surrogates for engaging in warfare with other nations. These surrogates (both state and non-state actors), he argued, might be employed to provoke international incidents to create alarm in an adversary; to destroy morale; to cause the diversion of an enemy's resources into security budgets; to effect specific forms of sabotage; to provoke repressive and reactive strategies; and the revolutionary over-throw of targeted regimes (what we may designate the Marighela (1971) strategy, that is, the provoking of indiscriminate responses – as applied by states rather than insurgent actors). In these cases the third party acts as a surrogate for the sponsoring state as the obvious effect and intent of the assistance provided is the improvement of the assisted actor's ability either to carry out terrorist actions to maintain a regime's rule or to create chaos and/or the eventual overthrow of an identified enemy-state regime. Thus, the Iranian government aided (and still aids) Hamas and Hezbollah; Syria has aided Hezbollah; prior to September 11 (and possibly after), Pakistan's security services were connected to Lashkar-e-Taiba (LET) and Harakat-ul-Mujahedeen terrorists in Kashmir; and Sudan and then Afghanistan provided safe haven for Al Qaeda, and the USA helped the mujahidin in Afghanistan, among many other examples. In most cases the state strives to keep these connections cov-ert so as to maintain plausible deniability with the hope of avoiding or at least deflecting and diminishing perceptions of direct responsibil-ity. In some cases the state assists in the establishment or the funding of an organization but does not involve itself with the actual opera-tions of the insurgent organization. As the November 2008 incident in Mumbai indicates, Lashkar-e-Taiba's historic connection to Pakistan now severely threatens Indo-Pakistani relations and demonstrates the negative consequences of such a strategy when the links between state and organization are revealed (Gordon, 2009).

It is important to recognize that in each of these forms of state terror, the capacities of the state, even poor states, greatly exceed the capacities of insurgents to operate within and across national boundaries. The assumptions of the Westphalian system of international relations, established in 1648, the core of which are bundled within the concept of national sovereignty, make the state the constituent unit of the global system and grant to it both the right to exercise its power within the boundaries of the state relatively unimpeded and to represent the state across national boundaries (with all attendant rights of diplomatic immunity and free movement of accompanying goods). As we shall discuss in the conclusion, these assumptions and rights make it much more difficult to confront state terror by the international community than for the community to confront and respond to instances of insurgent terror which threaten not only the populations of states but the formal constituent unit, the state itself.

State crime parasites and predators

As indicated above, there are numerous cases of state criminal activities and numerous forms that the activities may take. As is the case with the state's employment of political terror, state rulers and officials engage in crime to advance their personal and political agendas. While state officials may use these activities to extend their political power, as with criminals operating outside the state apparatus the primary motive which distinguishes their activities from terrorists is that they seek to amass personal wealth rather than, or in addition to, achieve political gain. There are numerous forms of the state–crime nexus that may occur depending upon the relative power of the state, its legitimacy within its own society, the circumstances of its historical creation and development and its geographic location and neighbors. In this section we discuss the conditions under which these activities are likely to occur and the implications of state crime for government and society.

The most common form of state crime is corruption. Corruption is endemic to political life and no form of government is immune. Ocampo (2002), following the lead of the OECD and World Bank, argues that 'corruption occurs when the agent (public employee) takes possession of some public benefit, either financial or of any other nature, and does not remit it to the principal' (national state). Criminal organizations seek to corrupt the state so that they may operate with less fear of interdiction and greater ease of operation. For the criminal, the bribe, payoff or if you will, tax, that is necessary to assure ease of operation is a cost of 'doing business.' There are many different forms of corruption that occur within states including:

- Buying political offices across the executive (including administrative offices), legislative and judicial branches

- Funding elections and appointments

- Bribery

  □ in procurement of contracts

  □ to ease smuggling of drugs, people and arms across borders

  □ to avoid payment of taxes

- Shifting public funds to private accounts

- Establishing safe havens (for persons and funds)

- To avoid penalties for regulatory infractions (environmental, employment, health and safety, etc.)

What distinguishes criminal states from others are both the state's capacity and willingness to combat or encourage corruption in its midst. Legitimate, strong and administratively competent states establish administrative agencies (often inspectors general) which monitor and analyze the functioning of contracts and grants, regulatory performance and the like to deter individual and systemic breakdowns into criminality. Criminal states, on the other hand, manage the opportunities and resources that such corruption can provide.

In Peru, Alberto Fujimori, democratically elected, presided over a government which 'normalized' corruption to the benefit of himself and the head of the intelligence services, Vladimiro Montesinos (Ocampo, 2002). They organized the trafficking of drugs and weapons in alliance with criminal organizations both within Peru and around the world.

Russia and Nigeria are two large states that have been particularly problematic. In Russia, following the collapse of the Soviet Union and the transition to a market economy, the acquisition of state assets by former party functionaries and well placed others was common: 'In effect organized crime has neutralized the criminal justice system, superseded some state functions, and captured parts of the state apparatus. The extent of the symbiosis between crime and politics warrants describing Russia as a captured state' (Williams, 2001: 113–114). Others refer to these state structures as crony capitalism (see Haber, 2002 for a discussion of Latin American crony capitalist states). In Nigeria under Abacha (1993–98), the state moved from being a 'passive beneficiary' to the initiator and controller of a significant segment of the nation's criminal activities with the proceeds flowing to the enrichment of Abacha and his cronies.[11]

The unholy alliance: states and organized crime

Nicolic-Ristanovic (1998) refers to the 'unholy alliance' established between politicians and organized crime which is given organizational form in ethnically-based paramilitary units. In a series of studies building upon this work, Mincheva and Gurr (2010; in press a; in press b) examine Bosnia, Albania and the Kurds and the implications for state crime and terrorist organizational connections. We will examine the network implications in the following chapter but here it is important to note the implications of the state–sovereignty connections to criminal activities.

Mincheva and Gurr (in press b) argue that in the case of Bosnia, the scarcity of weaponry, combined with an arms embargo imposed on the former Yugoslavia meant that the Bosnians had to not only work with Islamic nations and charities for material assistance, they also had to violate the embargo and employ various sub-state and criminal organizations to move the weapons to Bosnia. States appear to engage frequently in illegal (i.e. criminal) activity with respect to arms and embargoes. In the United States the origins of the Iran–Contra affair during the Reagan administration involved a complicated set of criminal and organizational operations. These combined a trade of arms to Iran

---

[11] There are interesting hybrid or partial cases, closer to home. See Scott (1969)

in return for Hezbollah-held hostages. Through additional 'unauthorized' activities, agents of the United States government (e.g. Oliver North) sought to circumvent congressional prohibitions (the Boland Amendment), and devised a mechanism for shifting residual funds to arm the Nicaraguan Contras (US Congress, 1987).

In April 2008 one of the world's most notorious arms traffickers, Viktor Bout, reputedly the model for Nicholas Cage's character in the film *Lord of War*, was arrested in Bangkok as a result of a DEA sting operation dedicated to targeting arms suppliers of the FARC (Revolutionary Armed Forces of Colombia). The same United States government had some years earlier hired Bout to transport weapons to the United States military in Iraq.

(A)s recently as August, Air Bas, a company tied to Bout and his associates, was flying charter missions under contract with the US military in Iraq. Air Bas is overseen by Victor Bout's brother, Sergei, and his long-time business manager, Richard Chichakli, an accountant living in Texas; in the past, payments for Air Bas have gone to a Kazakh company that the United Nations identifies as a front for the leasing operations of Victor Bout's aircraft. (Scherer, 2004)

By no means is the mix of criminal activities and the state, with respect to arms, limited to strong powerful states and states at war. As Farah (2004) argues, in Charles Taylor's Liberia, 'international arms dealers worked alongside Al Qaeda operatives, Israeli and South African mercenaries, Hezbollah diamond merchants, and Russian and Balkan organized crime figures' and thus Taylor both bankrupted and stripped the Liberia state of its resources, while amassing a personal fortune. Taylor, employing the state for his own personal use, was able to enjoy the internationally recognized benefits of sovereignty (passports, chartering of companies – particularly trading and shipping companies, and the collection of taxes for his personal use rather than state functions) and in so doing to not only threaten his own countrymen with his power internally but also to enable criminals and terrorists to benefit from the privileges they could purchase from him to the detriment of other nations. Interestingly, as was so often the case during the 1990s, one of the beneficiaries of Taylor's Liberia was Viktor Bout, who also sold and transported weapons to the Taliban in Afghanistan, rebel forces in Sierra Leone, to the Congo and Rwanda among others.

These forms of state crime, whether they be the institutionalization of corrupt practices in an otherwise functioning state or the infrequent tolerance of corrupt practices in the service of what government officials consider the momentary 'national interest' rather than simply for pecuniary gain, all serve to undermine the authoritative role of the state and the legitimacy of state institutions. As UN Secretary General Ban Ki-moon (2007) has argued, 'Corruption undermines democracy and the rule of law. It leads to violations of human rights. It erodes public trust in government. It can even kill – for example, when corrupt officials allow medicines to be tampered with, or when they accept bribes that enable terrorist acts to take place.'

As a consequence, corruption can result in security risks at national, regional and global levels. Transparency International, a non-governmental organization established to publicize corruption and lobby for means to combat it, argues that over time corruption in its various forms including bribery, money laundering, illegal tax havens and other criminal activities, serves to threaten the ability of the state to command the loyalty of its ordinary citizens. Abraham and van Schendel (2005: 14) contend that 'individuals and social groups that systematically contest or bypass state controls do not simply flout the letter of the law; with repeated transgressions over time, they bring into question the legitimacy of the state itself by questioning the state's ability to control its own territory.' To illustrate in the context of the contemporary situation in Afghanistan, the ongoing failure of the United States, NATO and the United Nations to bring security and stability to Afghanistan since the overthrow of the Taliban is not the result simply of incomplete military operations. A significant part of the story is the inability of the state to bring under control the corruption and criminality of its governmental officials and tribal leaders. Transparency International reports that Afghanistan fell from its position as the 117th most corrupt nation to 176 of 180 most corrupt on its Corruption Perceptions Index (on this index the lowest is most corrupt). The result has been increases in poppy production, a resurgent Taliban, and most importantly a severe decline in the Afghan people's support of the Karzai government which had been installed as a result of the overthrow of the Taliban in 2001. Its ultimate viability remains uncertain.

In the next chapter we will explore the nexus between criminals and terrorist groups and the role of the state as combatant, participant, and passive and active beneficiary.

FOUR

intersections of terrorist and criminal organizations

Introduction

It has long been argued that there are 'growing' links between terrorists and criminals. More recently the concern has been the growing connection between what have been labeled transnational criminal networks and global terrorism networks. This chapter addresses both the links between criminals and terrorists and the potential overlap and meshing of their networks. Criminals and terrorists may engage in similar activity (such as money laundering, bank robberies and smuggling). Terrorist groups may engage in conventional criminal activity in furtherance of fund raising. Criminal organizations may engage in terrorist activity such as assassination, and can engage in ideologically motivated violence. The two types may relate symbiotically, as when they exchange drugs for weapons. The fluid environment within which terrorist and organized crime groups operate provides both threats and opportunities. The development of networked organizational forms by both terrorist and conventional criminal organizations has enhanced both their capacity and their resilience. Both types of organizations use new technologies to support their operations, or as targets of crime.

As we explore these illicit organizations, we will consider their abilities at adaptive behaviors in the new environments in which they find themselves as a result of both government pursuit and changing global conditions. As we consider the intersections between terrorists and criminals and the actions they commit, it is necessary to remember the important distinctions between terrorism and crime. These distinctions have significant implications for confronting terrorism and criminality within communities, which we will explore in Chapter 6.

In the past two decades the possibilities and realities of the growing connections between terrorists and criminals – and in more recent years, between criminal networks and terrorist networks – have begun to concern both authorities and scholars. Some scholars worried that the Soviet Union was sponsoring narco-terrorism in various parts of the globe. For example, on January 28, 1987 Rachel Ehrenfeld argued in a lecture to the Heritage Foundation that 'The Soviet Union with the collaboration of its allies in Eastern Europe, Asia, and the Western Hemisphere is the initiator and sponsor of major narco-terrorist activities' (Ehrenfeld, 1987). While there was great dispute about the Soviet role in both the areas of state sponsorship of terrorism and connections to criminal activities, with the end of the Cold War scholars argued that the resultant decline in state sponsorship of terrorist activity has been responsible for the increasing turn to criminal activity by terrorists in order to replace the lost revenue previously supplied by states to groups who were seen as proxies for the battle between East and West (see for example Makarenko, 2004; Hutchinson, and O'Malley, 2007; Dishman, 2005; Hamm, 2005; Hoffman, 1998). At the same time, globalization, and the dramatic impact of the information revolution have enabled communication, command and control capabilities to link geographically separated individuals and groups inexpensively and immediately around the globe. Consequently, organizations develop greater reach and greater opportunities to develop more complicated networks of action.

The post-September 11 climate also altered the political environment in which many criminal and terrorist organizations operated, focusing greater attention on, and heightening concern over, their range of activities. In this new environment states began to seek, alone or in cooperation with other states, to eliminate perceived safe havens for terrorist operations and to reduce the capacity for illicit groups to use the global financial system to finance their activities. The increasing investment by states in counter terrorism and the application of military power to the problem of terrorism also greatly impacted the operating environment for criminals and terrorists and their points of intersection. The resultant decline in state funding sources and the consequence of some of the counter terrorism successes (particularly with respect to the cut-off of the easy flow of funds through money laundering and charities), as well as eroding the organizational capacity of some of these organizations, has led to a search by some terrorist groups for 'activities' to fund their organizations, because some cells have been cut off from direct organizational financial support (see for example Dishman, 2005).

Terrorists and criminals

Common activities

Although human motivation is complex, and motives often mixed, the basic distinction between terrorism and criminality has long been seen as rooted in the motivations for the behaviors that constitute terrorist or criminal acts. Thus, conventional criminals tend to be in it for the money, while terrorists seek political change. In a well known typology Hacker (1976) distinguished between criminals, crazies and crusaders when attempting to distinguish the motives behind violent acts. In general, criminals are motivated by greed; 'crazies' are characterized by mental instability, and crusaders by what they see as a moral imperative.

Remember that terrorism is communicatively constituted violence for political ends. The violence of the act (or the threat of such violence) is intended to send a message about fear and harm and to threaten and coerce the political audience – both government and public. Criminals use violence to accomplish tactical objectives in pursuit of a pecuniary goal. Terrorists wish to intimidate governments to gain political concessions; criminals wish to intimidate or coerce to gain financial rewards. The lines between terrorists and criminals are often blurred, because members of political and criminal organizations may use the tactics associated with the other type of organization to accomplish their goals. When we define organizations as terrorist there is a tendency to define all the acts undertaken by those organizations and in support of those organizations as terrorist (and correspondingly, for criminal organizations). While both types of organizations and actors seek to avoid capture, criminal organizations within stable political environments are more likely to value continuity. Governments can be corrupted in order to provide a more predictable adversary. By contrast, terrorist organizations seek the overthrow of governments and value unstable governments that they can more easily challenge. The relationship between Al Qaeda and the Taliban in pre 9/11 Afghanistan is an important exception, but it is so because Al Qaeda directed its terrorism outside the borders of Afghanistan and was in a symbiotic rather than competitive relationship with the Taliban state. Whether as an end in itself or as a means of supporting terrorist activity, theft may be common to both types of illicit organization. In addition, both criminals and terrorists may have an interest in concealing the origins of those assets they have at their disposal because a 'money trail' may be a very convenient way for governments to track them down.

Confusion may also arise because terrorists are frequently charged under criminal statutes and officials seek to demean political motives by suggesting that the terrorist is 'little more than a common criminal.' This is possibly due to the fact that some terrorists have indeed transformed into criminal organizations and likewise, some criminals use terrorism under specific circumstances. Organized crime groups for example have attacked representatives of the state when the authorities became too aggressive. One sees this for example in attacks against 'overzealous' prosecutors who do not accept the status quo (under which a blind eye is turned to corruption and crime). But the terror tactics by the mafia to subvert anti-mafia actions by the Italian judiciary should not lead us to define the Mafia as a terrorist organization, as its purpose in using such tactics is to impede criminal justice – not to alter the basic political system which it favors because it is characterized by a comfortable level of corruption. Moreover, most contemporary systems of jurisprudence do not recognize 'political' crimes as distinct from 'purely' criminal acts. Governments may portray acts that terrorists conceive as political acts as criminal activities with purely individual motives. The government's purpose in linking terrorists to criminals is to deny any possible 'legitimacy' of their motives or actions with the population they are trying to influence, by arguing that by definition, their actions are outside the political processes and by implication for personal rather than political gain.

Governments (and others) may also label criminals as terrorists in order to inflate their threat – thus the creation of the term 'narco-terrorists' and the rhetorical and consequential military strategy contained in the declaration of a War on Drugs long before the present War on Terror commenced (see Miller and Damask, 1996). More recently, Sanderson (2004: 50) notes that the US State Department's list of designated foreign terrorist organizations (FTOs) indicates that 14 of the 36 FTOs now traffic in narcotics. In addition to the implications of this for understanding the intersection of criminal and terrorist networks which we discuss below, there are also of course disputes about the quality of information that ties some of the designated groups to the narcotics trade. For example, David Kaplan of *US News and World Report* reported that counter-terrorism officials disputed reports of bin Laden's involvement in the drug trade, calling them 'flat wrong.' It has also been reported that Al Qaeda officials have encouraged their members not to get involved with drug traffickers because they don't trust the traffickers (more on this below).

Nonetheless there is no doubt that there are intersections between terrorists and criminals: terrorists often commit crimes, and criminals employ terror (although less frequently than terrorists commit non-political crimes). Some observers contend that the new post-Cold War environment and the development of a networked organization are at the root of much of the pressure for terrorists to turn into criminals. For example, Treverton et al. (2009) argue that as state sponsorship and private philanthropy dry up, crime becomes a more common source of terrorist finance. Organizations which have employed terrorism have engaged in clearly criminal activities for many years. Lohamei Herut Israel ('Fighters for the Freedom of Israel'), also known as the Stern Gang, robbed a bank in Tel Aviv in 1940 in order to obtain funds to finance their activities. At the height of the Troubles, banks in Northern Ireland were regularly robbed by paramilitary groups on both sides of the religious divide as a means of topping up their coffers. The PLO's Force 17, the Japanese Red Army, and the Baader Meinhof gang or Rote Armee Faktion all conducted bank robberies during the Cold War. And more recently, the white supremacist group, The Aryan Republican Army (ARA) led by Peter Langan and composed of five other core members, robbed a total of 22 Midwestern banks in the United States between 1994 and 1996. But terror organizations have not limited their criminal activities to robbing banks. Hezbollah sympathizers in Latin America have donated millions of dollars to the organization with proceeds of various profitable criminal activities including CD piracy, drug dealing and extortion (Treverton et al., 2009: 75). In 2002 Hezbollah operatives, smuggling pseudoephedrine for the production of methamphetamines, were arrested in 'Operation Mountain Express' by US and Canadian authorities. Dishman also claims that Hezbollah had established a long-standing criminal alliance with Mexican drug dealers from which they netted millions of dollars that were then laundered and sent to the Middle East (Dishman, 2005: 247).

Morphogenesis

Terrorist groups have been known to transform themselves into criminal organizations, and vice versa. The Abu Sayaf Group (ASG) in the Philippines began its life as a terrorist organization whose main goal was the establishment of a separate state for the minority Muslim population of the Philippines. Although it purports to continue toward this goal today, since the death of its founder Abdurajik Abubakar Janjalani in 1998, the group has engaged in many ransom-driven kidnappings and many criminals have emerged in key leadership positions. It appears that the group's political identity has been subordinated to the quest for profit, with the number of kidnappings dramatically rising after the death of Janjalani.

The Islamic Movement of Uzbekistan (IMU) had a similar process of metamorphosis. The group emerged with the stated goal of overthrowing the secular Uzbek state and establishing Islamic rule in Central Asia. As with ASG, it too lost one of its leaders, Juam Namaganly, and it appears that the organization's priorities shifted more to the criminal end of the Makarenko continuum with many of its activities devoted to the drug trade and control of smuggling routes in the region (see Rosenthal, 2008: 284).

Many terrorism analysts claim that the Revolutionary Armed Forces of Colombia (FARC) is still motivated primarily by ideology (see for example Peceny and Durnan, 2006), true to its origins as a revolutionary Marxist–Leninist group. However, since the 1980s it has engaged in the cocaine trade to finance itself. The Colombian Government claims that the FARC is now the world's richest terrorist group with hundreds of millions of dollars in revenue stemming from the drug trade, extortion, and kidnapping. FARC earns approximately $91.6 million yearly in kidnappings alone. As FARC's income has grown in the past two decades, it apparently has spent relatively little of the funds on weapons, training and revolutionary activities, leading some to argue that 'the group's grand strategic objective is making money' (Rosenthal, 2008: 487).

D Company, led by Dawood Ibrahim, began as a drug dealing organization in Mumbai, India and has expanded to be a major criminal organization in the Indian subcontinent, though Ibrahim relocated to Dubai in the 1980s to manage smuggling operations. Its operations include arms, drugs, money laundering, Bollywood piracy and the transport of the foregoing. In a climate of strained relations between Indian Muslims and Hindus, and after the Hindu gangs destroyed the Babri Mosque in the city of Ayodhya and rioting that resulted in about 2000 mostly Indian Muslim deaths in 1992, Ibrahim organized the 1993 terrorist bombings in Mumbai which killed 257 people. D Company is now considered to be closely linked with Lashkar-e-Taiba (LET), the 'army of the pure,' a Pakistan based terrorist organization which also first emerged in the aftermath of the 1992 anti Muslim riots. LET seeks not only the 'restoration' of Kashmir to Pakistan but also has a more expansive agenda of restoring Islamic rule over all of India and the creation of Islamic rule across the entire subcontinent.

Organized criminals as terrorists

In some situations, organized criminals will employ terrorist tactics to further their ends. In so doing, they will employ violence in order to create an acquiescent public, or directly against agents of the state to effect policy change.

The Mafia assassinations of Judges Falcone and Borsellino with truly massive bombs were noted in Chapter 1. Designed to intimidate Sicilian authorities, these killings had the unintended consequences of provoking public revulsion and support for increased law enforcement powers. As we will discuss in Chapter 6, authorities need not only to take advantage of the public's backlash in such situations, they must also create opportunities through policy campaigns to create the conditions under which a backlash is more likely against criminals and terrorists.

Among the more prominent recent examples of political terrorism on the part of criminal organizations are the work of drug gangs in Colombia and Mexico. In 2008, more than 60 police officers in Ciudad Juarez, Mexico were killed by drug trafficking groups, some by beheading. The following year, the Chief of Police resigned after the murders of several more officers, and the threat that a police officer would be killed every 48 hours until he stepped down (Ellingwood, 2009). The success of such intimidation by criminal organizations threatens the stability of the state and thus becomes a political as well as judicial problem – as if their original aim was as the terrorist to decrease the trust of the community in the state's ability to maintain its primacy of power.

Illicit organizations may also engage in vertical integration, complementary to other activities such as trafficking, or horizontal expansion in which they search for new lines of business. Both criminal and terrorist organizations survive by adapting to a changing environment. This can entail the exploitation of new and emerging technologies in furtherance of their organizational goals and/or abandoning old ways of doing business when they become too risky or are no longer profitable. Digital technology, for example, has become more powerful, much less costly, and widely accessible in recent years. It permits perfect duplication and dissemination of computer software, DVDs and music, from remote locations far and wide. The piracy of such content yields rich rewards at relatively low risk. Barriers to entry and overhead costs are insignificant, and enforcement priorities often allow pirates to operate with impunity (Treverton et al., 2009: 116). Thus, for example, the Japanese Boryokudan experienced declining revenues from pornographic DVDs when that type of content became widely available on the internet. They quickly moved into video piracy. Russian criminals have also been adaptable. The privatization of state owned assets in Russia enabled criminal interests to gain ground-floor access to legitimate enterprises – and thus to exploit them for illicit purposes. Recognizing that India's trade liberalization and the relaxation of import duties made smuggling for the purpose of the evasion of customs duties no longer feasible, Dawood Ibrahim's D Company stopped smuggling precious metals and electronic products, and turned to video piracy. As Indian law discouraged private financing of the film industry, Ibrahim was also able to engage in the extortionate financing of film production.

Networks

Increasingly, the literature on transnational criminal organizations and terrorism has been concerned with the development of organizational networks between and among these organizations. Both criminal organizations and terrorist organizations have sought to exploit new communication technologies and global mechanisms for finances, and like many other organizations have made use of the principles of networks. However, this in and of itself does not create overlapping terrorist and criminal networks. Few would dispute the existence of working relations among some terrorist groups and criminal facilitators which result in relatively low-level cooperation through financial transactions for services regarding safe houses, travel documents, weapons, information and the like. The important questions for us are whether these 'networks' of information sharing or service relations extend to the actual networking of the terrorist groups with criminal organizations; whether these interactions imply any coordinated effort toward long-term organizational alliances, mergers or transformations, and if so, what are the implications for law enforcement and the state.

Networks may be understood as temporary, dynamic, emergent, adaptive, entrepreneurial and flexible structures which often arise out of exchange relationships among organizations. Depending on the zone of their operations, they may cross-national boundaries and therefore operate in many different social milieux and in very different ways. When these organizations attempt to cross-national borders they confront the same linguistic, cultural and social prejudices, suspicions and historical contexts that all 'globalizing' entities encounter.

The term network has been used for over 200 years, at first designating a structural feature which enabled connections among physical locations. In general, we find that network organizations are less hierarchical and thus flatter than traditional organizations. Quite often connections are built and dissolved based upon the needs for achieving the mission/tasks of the organizations. As a result, organizations in short-term strategic alliances in which they otherwise maintain their independence as organizations are often misleadingly labeled as networks.

A strategic or tactical alliance represents an intentionally and formally prescribed linkage created between two or more organizations. Williams reminds us that:

> Networks vary in size, shape, membership, cohesion and purpose. Networks can be large or small, local or global, domestic or transnational, cohesive or diffuse, centrally directed or highly decentralized, purposeful or directionless. A specific network can be narrowly and tightly focused on one goal or broadly oriented toward many goals, and it can be either exclusive or encompassing in its membership. (1999: 65)

Within the terrorism literature, the 'organization as network' appeared as early as 1977 with the publication of Ovid Demaris's *Brothers in Blood: the International Terrorist Network* (1977), followed by the publication of Claire Sterling's (1981) widely cited (and often quite properly excoriated) exposé *The Terror Network* (see Stohl, 1983). These authors argued that terrorist groups had established worldwide liaisons and networks, securing cooperation among national and international terrorist organizations and some states in the form of common financial and technical support. Stohl and Stohl (2007: 95) have argued that the two central problems in this early terror network literature are still apparent today. First, in spite of the inherent dynamism and emergent flexibility embedded in the term network, public policy makers viewed terrorist networks as hierarchically organized and centralized bureaucracies. Second, the clandestine nature of terrorist networks enabled political opportunism to compromise the reliability and validity of the declared networks' boundary specifications, and the nature of the linkages amongst the organizations thus cast doubt on many of the subsequent conclusions. Clearly, it will always be the case that when dealing with clandestine organizational networks, the validity of the network data will be in question as even the most careful intelligence agencies and law enforcement officials around the world will have to make assumptions and draw connections from very incomplete and suspect data.

The solution to the dilemma of boundary specification lies in our ability to identify the constitutive features of organizational communication in terms of coordination, control and membership integration – the collaborative interface which results in a systemic structure that is meaningful and recognizable. In short it is necessary to be able to distinguish operating in the same spaces that networks operate, the ability 'to network,' (i.e., the structural capacity to activate the ubiquitous six degrees of separation) and the ability to mobilize, control and coordinate members for specific planned acts. This means that not all acts of mobilization are equal in their meaning. For example, many terrorist groups arose in the context of longstanding political or ethnic grievances and conflicts. These grievances may have long histories and political parties, and community organizations may be addressing the issues through normal legal and non-violent channels. They may be connected to media organizations that favor their political position. Many citizens may support these parties and be willing to vote for candidates who represent their identity based goals and aspirations. All of these components may be able to be mobilized as a network of supporters – some of whom may have 'official' links with the political party. Such organizations can mobilize their 'network of supporters' for various activities but it would not make sense to think of them as part of the organizational command structure. Thus it is important to recognize that connections do not equal coordination; temporary exchange relationships do not equal control; and identification of an agreed enemy does not equal the emergence of an organization. Perhaps the most important differences among groups are the nature of their goals and therefore the purpose of the violence they employ.

When we are considering the question of terrorist or criminal networks as well as their intersections it is worth noting that the importance of these linkages is not predicated simply on the number of links that send or receive information but on the sustained capacity of the organization to carry out its chosen aims through those links. As Hoffman argues, the importance of these links for terrorists is whether it helps them 'to mobilize and to animate both actual and would be fighters, supporters, and sympathizers' (Hoffman, 2003: 434).

Makarenko's (2004: 131) seven point crime–terror continuum may be employed to identify the intersections between criminals and terrorists. From the 'organized crime' end of the continuum, one moves through 1) alliances with terrorist groups; 2) use of terror tactics for operational purposes; 3) political crime; in the centre one finds 4) the 'Black Hole' Syndrome, where the two types converge. Moving toward the terrorism end, one encounters 3) commercial terrorism; 2) criminal activities for terrorist operational purposes, and 1) alliance with criminal organisations. The seven points on the continuum may be divided into four general groups: alliances, operational motivations, convergence and the black hole. Bjornehed (2004: 311) suggests that 'the organisations along the crime-terror continuum are often dependent on the same suppliers, means of transport, infrastructure and source of income.' In short, because they often operate in the same physical as well as cyber geography of facilitators, crime hubs and safe havens, members of these organizations may both 'innocently' as well as purposefully converge.

Mincheva and Gurr (2010, in press a, in press b) in a series of studies examining what they label as the unholy alliances between transnational terrorists and crime networks, posit four general types of terrorist–crime connections based on the motivation and circumstances that drive terrorists' interest in criminal activities and whether terrorists evolve into criminals. These four factors are *ideological*: in which primacy is given to ideological objectives and illicit economic activities are undertaken to fund political programs; *pragmatic*: in which a 'pragmatic shift' in a terrorist organization's agenda takes place such that political goals are not abandoned but material gain becomes a major objective; *predatory*: in which the political militants' agenda shifts entirely away from political objectives toward material gain; and *opportunistic interdependence*: in which political goals and material gain co-exist on an equal footing and a political–criminal hybrid organization emerges.

First, the ideological can be illustrated by the Bosnians who 'turned to Islamic countries and charities for material assistance following the international recognition of Bosnia's independence when the near simultaneous imposition of an arms embargo on the former Yugoslavia left the Bosniaks with little weaponry.' Second, terrorists may be pragmatically driven. This evidently is the case with the FARC of Colombia, which forged alliances of convenience with drug dealers. This not only gained funds for their insurgency but also turned FARC into a long-term business activity. In pursuit of material gain terrorists can lose focus on politics and evolve into 'fighters turn felons.' Thirdly, the Algerian Islamists turned into 'social bandits'; their connection with crime has been characterized as predation. Finally, militants can be simultaneously terrorists and criminals, as is the case with some ethnic Albanian factions. This pattern is what we call opportunistic interdependence' (Mincheva and Gurr, in press a: 2–3).

A recent example of what appears to be pragmatic networking is found in the 2009 Pakistani police accusation that the Taliban is working with criminal groups and using Mafia-style networks to kidnap, rob banks and extort within the southern Pakistani city of Karachi, generating millions of dollars for the militant insurgency (which employs numerous terrorist acts) in northwestern Pakistan.

Ironically, we also often find agents of states converging in these same crime hubs. States may find themselves dependent upon the same networks, as revealed by the case of notorious international arms dealer (mentioned above), Victor Bout. Bout, operating within a network of legal corporations registered in the United States and numerous European, African and Asian nations, developed an extraordinary logistics and transportation network through which he purchased and transported both illicit and licit cargos. (Indeed as Farrah and Braun (2007) discovered, it was Bout's entrepreneurship that encouraged him to extend his operations to various legal cash crops. He was thus able to avoid bringing home empty the airplanes that had illegally delivered arms to dozens of countries, dramatically increasing his profitability.) Bout's success and 'reliability' in delivering to difficult and remote areas led the US government to contract with him during the initial stages of the War in Iraq. As Stephen Braun (2007) writes,

Bout turned up as a linchpin in the US supply line to Iraq. Air Force records obtained by *The Times* show that his planes flew hundreds of runs into the high-security zone at Baghdad International Airport, delivering everything from guns to drilling equipment to frozen food for customers from the US Army to mega-contractor KBR Inc.

Trust

Trust is a chronic problem for any clandestine organization, including both organized crime and terrorist organizations. Therefore, such organizations, in their efforts to avoid penetration and thus survive, will carefully screen in their recruitment patterns, relying on strong rather than weak ties, and often demanding a test of loyalty or fidelity (requiring the commitment of a crime to demonstrate bona fides) (Gambetta 2009, chapter 2).

To deal with the issue of trust, some networks are built upon relational homophily (family, friends, and identity). Comparisons of ethnically-based terrorist organizations such as Hamas, Hezbollah and the Basque ETA with multi-ethnic terrorist groups such as Al Qaida and Aum Shinri-kyo (responsible for the Sarin nerve gas attack on the Tokyo subway) also point out the critical importance of distinguishing between global and local networks. Hamas and other ethnically-based organizations enact a cell structure composed primarily of homophilous links (e.g. clan or ethnic group members). Constructed as typical cell organizations, growth and preferential attachment are turned inward. Conspirators do not form many new ties outside the network and often minimize the activation of existing ties inside the network. Strong ties, which remain mostly dormant and hidden, were frequently formed years ago within the family and local community as well as in school and training camps, and keep the cell interconnected. Many such organizations only recruit their members from a known and rather closed circle of potential participants, for example the family or clan and thus rely on kinship ties to provide trust (see Norton, 1988: 3). Observers have noted that within the Lebanese Shi'a fundamentalist group Hezbollah, members are not only connected by their religious ties but also that the subgroups within Hezbollah are often linked through close family blood ties as well. Much the same connections are also found in the group Amal, a faction of Hezbollah many of whose members are from the Musawi clan.

Williams (1999: 70–72) discusses both the 'embedded ties' and enduring relations which are based on high levels of trust, mutual respect, and mutual concern as well as the temporary relations based on nothing more than a momentary coincidence of interests. 'In many cases, bonding will be directly related to family or kinship: Many Italian Mafia groups are still organized along family lines, while Turkish drug trafficking and criminal organizations are often clan based. Other bonding mechanisms include ethnicity and common experience in which the participants develop a strong sense of trust and mutual reliance.' Williams (1999: 75) further argues that such criminal networks, located in ethnic communities, offer cover, concealment and a constant supply of recruits. When those ethnic communities stretch across national borders, a strategic alliance between criminal and terrorist groups may develop. For example, Makarenko (2004) discusses how Albanian criminal organizations used their criminal profits to purchase arms and military equipment for the Kosovo Liberation Army. The Albanian ethnic national religious identification motivated the criminal organizations to assist their cross border political 'brethren.'

It is important to note that there are important inhibitors of terrorist and criminal intersections. Rosenthal (2008: 490) argues that terrorists and criminals rarely cooperate because they prefer developing their own group's capabilities to allying with untrustworthy groups with ostensibly different priorities. Part of the issue for terrorists is that they are wary of being seen as 'simply criminal' actors because it may delegitimize their political mission. Criminals, on the other hand, worry about associations with terrorists because they may thereby be seen as providing a far more direct challenge to the legitimacy of the state and call forth a much greater state response and increasing public demands for action than if they were merely seen as acting for pecuniary gain.

Interestingly, as Hutchinson and O'Malley (2007) remind us, entrenched organized crime organizations are often highly nationalistic. Thus the Yakuza and the Mafia, for example, are likely to consider only certain types of one offs, and/or short- or long-term alliances for possible relationships. The more tightly the entrenched organization is structured, the more likely such organizational dynamics will prevail.

It is possible to build networks based upon the homophily of a particular value and 'like-mindedness.' If terrorist organizations and criminal organizations agree to cooperate, they are likely to do so by identifying the similarities (as well as potential benefits) that have brought them together while at the same time they recognize the potential conflicts inherent in their organizational missions and structures. While such networks may be possible to construct, it is also the case that they are far more fragile than those based upon ties built upon 'embedded trust.' Thus, scholars of terrorism have long been aware that the terrorist networks that have endured over time are tied to ethno-nationalist or communal struggles, protracted conflicts, political events and perceived historic grievances and inequalities. Likewise, the intersections of criminals and terrorists likely to have the best chance of originating and/or surviving will be those networks that arise out of these types of shared community. Morselli et al. (2007) remind us that organizations, both criminal and terrorist in origin, prefer to remain on the periphery of the continuum as a way of protecting themselves. They cite Baker and Faulkner (1993), who argue that clandestine networks are likely to pursue a tactical one time or very short connection, rather than a merger or clear alliance to reduce the chances of penetration. Morselli et al. also cite Erickson's (1981) studies of clandestine networks, which stressed that network members relied primarily on pre-existing networks that formed the foundation upon which each secret society was designed (i.e. strong ties) to compensate for risk when interacting with external individuals and groups. As mentioned earlier in the chapter, Al Qaeda strategists worried that drug trafficking would expose them to possible detection and the Al Qaeda leadership does not trust many of the big drug barons (see Kaplan, 2005).

Havens for illicit organizations

Criminal or terrorist groups may take refuge in locations where they are free from the scrutiny of law enforcement or security agencies. In some situations, this freedom may be bought, through bribery. Drug gangs in Mexico have flourished in part because officials have been paid to ignore them. In other circumstances, freedom from scrutiny may be gained when the group emerges from or takes refuge in locations where authorities are unconcerned, incompetent or nonexistent. As noted above, it is not coincidental that maritime piracy flourishes off the coast of Somalia, where there has been no effective government for nearly two decades. Of course, the governments of Sudan and subsequently, Afghanistan, tolerated Al Qaeda activities on their soil for considerable periods.

FIVE

responding to terrorism and organized crime: local, national and international dimensions

Introduction

State responses to terrorism and organized crime may vary from ruthless repression (from incapacitation of individuals through imprisonment, up to and including assassination) through a variety of incentives and inducements for desistance, to reintegration of the offender.

Some public policies achieve stunning success. Others fail miserably. Some produce mixed results, meeting some goals but not others. And some become noteworthy for their adverse unintended consequences – what some commentators refer to as 'blowback' or 'collateral damage.' The annals of organized crime and of terrorism contain abundant examples of all of these.

This chapter explores the implications and consequences of different state policy and operational approaches to confronting crime and terror. To do so we examine the political choices and impacts of 'war fighting' as opposed to criminal justice, and unilateral as distinct from multilateral approaches to the two types of challenge. There are considerable differences in policing systems across nations, and we thus discuss the constitutional arrangements that bear upon national versus local law enforcement responsibilities.

We also explore the consequences of responses that rely on public mobilization strategies, both those of a more reasoned kind, as well as the production of moral panics and the manipulation of fear. The independent role of the media in fostering a climate of fear is additionally noteworthy. A common strategy of governments seeks to delegitimize illicit organizations. Unfortunately, policies to this end may be ineffective or counterproductive. Ironically, careless actions by illicit organizations may be even more effective in eroding their own public support.

War fighting vs criminal justice

As we noted earlier, the metaphor of war is often employed by governments in order to mobilize their publics in furtherance of a policy objective. The War on Drugs and the War on Terror are the most obvious examples. Conventional wartime mobilization is usually accompanied by a call for material sacrifice (e.g. forgoing 'butter' to afford 'guns'), as well as a call to sacrifice other values, such as freedom of movement and freedom of expression.

Although the threats posed by both terrorism and organized crime are real, there remains the risk that governments may seek to overstate them for political advantage, or that law enforcement and/or security agencies may do so in order to acquire additional power and resources.

There are two major challenges facing contemporary democracies as they seek to control organized crime and terrorism. The first is that they ensure that the response to a threat is commensurate with the objective severity of that threat. The second is that they avoid responses that themselves compromise the fundamental values of human rights and the rule of law.

In both peace and war, government efforts to mobilize public support for a policy may entail the explicit choice to employ misinformation. During the Vietnam War, for example, the Kennedy, Johnson and Nixon Administrations were selective in their disclosures, arguably withholding information on the integrity of the South Vietnamese government and its armed forces, and on progress of the war in general, which might have allowed the American public to come to a more informed judgment about the wisdom of continuing the war effort. In 2002 President Bush proclaimed that Al Qaeda terrorists were active in Iraq, an assertion intended to justify the forthcoming invasion of that country. Ironically, the destruction of the Iraqi state following the downfall of Saddam Hussein actually attracted Al Qaeda sympathizers to the country. Tom Ridge, the former US Secretary of Homeland Security has claimed that he was pressured by the White House to raise the national threat level just prior to the 2004 Presidential election (Baker, 2009).

The old saying 'all's fair in love and war' is patently incorrect. A great deal of international law is devoted to limiting what combatants can do to each other when nations go to war. Governments that profess to embrace the rule of law are placed in a difficult position when confronted by organized crime and terrorism. Most democratic societies are bound by laws guaranteeing the rights of criminal suspects, and of those formally charged with crime. The laws of warfare, such as those embodied in the Geneva Conventions, are intended both to protect civilian noncombatants and prisoners of war, and to prohibit certain practices such as torture, the taking of hostages, and the use of poison gas. Those who transgress these prohibitions may find themselves liable to prosecution for war crimes. Nor is the adage at all appropriate when one is speaking about terrorism or organized crime. Of course, not all governments or their agents feel thus constrained and many constrained or not, are tempted to fight fire with fire.

Traditionally, terrorist activities that are undertaken by non-state actors have been considered as covered by conventional criminal law. In the aftermath of the terrorist attacks on September 11, 2001, the geographical dispersion of persons suspected of terrorist activity meant that they were often captured beyond the frontiers of the United States, either by host governments or by US agents. The Bush administration regarded it as advantageous to confer an ambiguous legal status on these individuals. As such, they were deemed to be neither prisoners of war (entitled to protection under the Geneva Conventions) nor common criminals, entitled to protection under the US Constitution (Mayer, 2008).

To further its war on terror, the Bush administration engaged in a number of actions of questionable legality, including the use of coercive interrogation techniques that amounted to torture (Bybee, 2002), and widespread interception of telecommunications without warrant (Congressional Research Service, 2006). The FBI made arguably inappropriate use of 'national security letters' to compel disclosure by companies of clients' consumer and financial information. The images from the Abu Ghraib prison and Guantanamo Bay not only offended friends of the United States, but actually created enemies (Donohue, 2008).

National vs local

The organization of policing in a given country usually reflects the structure of that country's government. In countries with a unitary governmental structure such as New Zealand, there is one national police service. In countries with federal systems of government, policing responsibilities are usually divided between a national police and police controlled by subordinate governmental units. Australia has a national police as well as separate police services for its six states and two self-governing territories. The United States, by contrast, has a variety of national law enforcement bodies, such as the FBI, the Drug Enforcement Administration, and the Secret Service, as well as over 10,000 separate police agencies at state, county, and municipal levels. Readers familiar with problems in organizational communication will appreciate that there are often impediments to information exchange, and to cooperation more generally, in one single organization. As one may imagine, communication problems are compounded when responsibility for law enforcement is shared horizontally and vertically across a plethora of separate organizations.

The challenge of terrorism has brought this into sharp relief. In the United States, the 9/11 Commission called attention to inadequate communication between the FBI and the CIA (National Commission on Terrorist Attacks Upon the United States, 2004). A smaller inquiry in Australia identified similar difficulties between law enforcement and intelligence agencies (Australian Federal Police, 2008). In the competitive world of policing and security, everyone wants to claim credit for a success, and deny responsibility for a failure.

One of the more significant challenges of counter-terrorism policing in federal systems is that of cooperation between national and local law enforcement agencies. Aside from the endemic challenges of inter-organizational rivalry and impediments to communication, relations may also be affected by differences in the respective roles of agencies at different levels of government. The jurisdiction of national police is usually limited to a small number of serious matters. In the case of terrorism, the potential harm may be catastrophic, and there may be very little time in which to prevent an incident or to contain one that has occurred. By contrast, local police deal with communities on a day-to-day basis, and depend upon the support or cooperation of local residents for their routine business. It is not difficult to imagine how relations between national and local law enforcement agencies can become strained (Thacher, 2005; Pickering et al., 2008). Jurisdictional rivalry may also characterize police response to organized crime. Rarely if ever in the criminal justice system of a federation is there a bright line demarcating those matters that are under the jurisdiction of national law enforcement organizations, and those which are the responsibility of local police. Offenders themselves do not set out to commit only federal crimes, to the exclusion of crimes that are offences under state law.

In the best of all possible worlds, police agencies would be guided by an operational, if not a legal, division of labor, and by carefully crafted memoranda of understanding that would provide for information sharing, joint operations and other collaborative arrangements as required. But in the real world, rivalries, jealousies, and mistrust can, and sometimes do, prevail.

Unilateral vs multilateral responses

In our era of globalization where people, finance, commodities and ideas travel around the world with unprecedented speed and volume, governmental responses to organized crime and terrorism usually require cooperation between nations across the globe. As we have discussed in previous chapters, supply chains for illicit goods and services often span oceans and continents; some terrorist activity may be 'home grown,' but much involves movement across national frontiers. This means that governments can't always 'go it alone.'

Even some of the most controversial aspects of the US government's response to terrorism required the cooperation or complicity of foreign states. The program of extraordinary rendition, where suspects were secretly transported for purposes of aggressive interrogation (to nations where such practices were legally or practically condoned) is illustrative (Congressional Research Service, 2009).

Although there is hardly a seamless web of international cooperation to combat organized crime and terrorism, there is a great deal of mutual support. This occurs bilaterally, between pairs of states, or multilaterally, across a number of states. Australia and Indonesia, for example, have entered into an agreement on a framework for security cooperation (Australia, Department of Foreign Affairs and Trade, 2006). Member states of the United Nations have agreed on a global strategy to counter terrorism (United Nations, 2008). At the regional and international levels there are multiple organizations which may provide important information resources and networks (e.g. Europol, Interpol) which are of use along with the security and police investigative services of individual nations.

Securitization and international competition

Despite these initiatives, there are still significant impediments to international cooperation in response to crime and terrorism. In the domain of conventional criminality, national priorities differ. For example, authorities in the United States regard software and entertainment piracy as serious. However, not all other countries share this concern. Accordingly, other governments who have competing domestic issues of an urgent nature may not have the resources or will to 'go the extra mile' to assist their US counterparts. Governments of stable, affluent nations often express great disquiet about people who seek to enter their countries illegally, and reserve particular opprobrium for those entrepreneurs ('people smugglers') who might profit from assisting them. Authorities in source countries such as Afghanistan or Sri Lanka, or transit countries such as Malaysia, or Albania, may not share these concerns.

International cooperation in matters of counterterrorism, as well as of organized crime, may be complicated by the tendency to 'securitize' these issues, that is, to treat them as existential threats or matters of national security. Where there are pre-existing political sensitivities between states, such as India and Pakistan, cooperation may be very difficult to achieve.

Intelligence

Intelligence has become a crucial tool in the response to crime and terrorism. The world learned on 9/11 that the failure to anticipate an impending threat can be catastrophic. The sources of intelligence can be quite varied. Information can be gleaned by direct observation, or by observation enhanced through technological means. Such methods can include photography or real time observation by aerial vehicles; listening devices; or global positioning technology, to name just a few. Suffice it to say that the growth of technological innovation will soon lead to intelligence methods as yet unforeseen. The increased volume of information already collected by intelligence and law enforcement agencies may pose greater challenges for criminals or terrorists, and for law abiding citizens who value privacy. Ironically, it has already begun to complicate the lives of intelligence officers themselves.

We noted above how impediments to the flow of information within and between organizations can contribute to continued ignorance of imminent threats. And the sheer volume of information collected by intelligence agencies can be daunting. In the aftermath of the 9/11 attacks, the United States spent billions of dollars re-organizing its intelligence systems to facilitate coordination of information derived from various sources. A National Counterterrorism Centre was created for just this purpose. However, the attempted bombing of an airliner in the US on Christmas Day 2009 revealed that a great deal remained to be achieved in this regard. The father of the would-be bomber had personally contacted the US Embassy in Nigeria to express concern about the increasing extremism of his son. Earlier, the US National Security Agency had intercepted communications in which Al Qaeda operatives in Yemen discussed the possibility of using a Nigerian in a future attack. But authorities failed to 'connect the dots' and the bombing was only thwarted when fellow passengers became aware of the offender's attempt to ignite something on his person, and restrained him.

Tensions between intelligence and investigation

Traditionally, the task of investigation is twofold: first, to determine 'who done it' and second, to assemble evidence sufficient to convict the accused in court. This applies to all criminal cases, whether they arise from ordinary crime or terrorism. By contrast, the fundamental purpose of intelligence is preventive: to determine that a crime or act of terrorism is likely to occur, so that it might be prevented. Law enforcement agents may become aware of a forthcoming crime because they have been 'tipped off' by an insider, or perhaps by an undercover agent. Incidents may also come to their attention as a result of covert surveillance or the interception of communications. As we have seen in the above anecdote, the challenge may be one of integrating two or more disparate pieces of information.

Of course, information obtained in furtherance of an investigation may also have immense intelligence value. The investigation that followed the 2002 Bali bombings led to the arrest of some 200 members of Jemaah Islamiyah, severely disrupting that organization.

Most nations have fairly exacting requirements governing the collection of intelligence and of evidence. These requirements are not always adhered to conscientiously. Some information with immense intelligence value may be inadmissible in court (should the terrorist act be prevented and the alleged perpetrators be charged with conspiracy or attempt) because it had been improperly collected. Some methods of investigation may also contribute to miscarriages of justice by producing what are referred to as 'false positives.' Aggressive means of interrogation, or outright torture, may lead a suspect to confess to a crime that he or she did not commit (Leo, 2008). So too can the fabrication of evidence by investigators, or the withholding of exculpatory evidence by investigators or prosecutors.

Strategies

Few individual members of illicit organizations, terrorist or criminal, are irreplaceable. A robust, resilient organization is capable of recruiting successors to those who fall by the wayside. It follows, therefore, that the conventional strategy of investigating and prosecuting individual members of a criminal or terrorist organization may be less successful than strategies of creating an inhospitable environment for the organization, or targeting the organization in a holistic and systematic way.

Prevention

Rather than wait until a criminal or terrorist act has been committed, authorities may take steps to reduce the likelihood of it occurring in the first place. According to routine activity theory, this will entail one or more policies or practices to a) reduce the supply of motivated offenders; b) reduce the number or vulnerability of prospective targets or victims; or c) to increase the extent of capable guardianship.

Reducing the supply of motivated offenders may entail a continuum of measures, ranging from the benign to the draconian. By introducing policies of social inclusion, governments such as the United Kingdom have sought to reduce the number of marginalized youth from ethnic minorities who might otherwise be recruited to criminal or terrorist organizations. Polices of social *exclusion* have also been employed. Most western industrial nations have tightened border control policies since the 9/11 attacks, making it more difficult for prospective foreign students or other visitors to obtain entry visas. Some countries deny visas to foreigners who have previously been convicted of a crime. Some have 'no-fly' lists, containing the names of potential terrorists who are prevented from embarking on aircraft. A more extreme example would involve the targeted assassination or imprisonment of potential terrorists.

Reducing the accessibility of targets or victims is perhaps the least fruitful policy option, in that it reduces the liberty of those whom the state wishes to protect. One cannot relocate the White House or the population of New York City. Rather, one can restrict the approachability of certain targets. Criminologists refer to this as target hardening. The erection of physical barriers has made it more difficult to deliver an explosives-laden truck to US embassies around the world. Similarly, the use of locked and reinforced cockpit doors in commercial aircraft has made pilots less vulnerable to attack (Clarke and Newman, 2006).

Capable guardianship through enhanced surveillance

As authorities accord increasing priority to organized crime, so governments mobilize an increasing array of measures. Among the more significant of these is the interception of telecommunications. All new technologies are vulnerable to exploitation by criminals, and communications technologies are no exception. The telephone and more recently the internet lend themselves nicely to communications in furtherance of criminal conspiracies. Indeed, the latter is ideally suited for communications across a geographically dispersed network. As governments became aware of the criminal misuse of communications technologies, they sought means of intercepting these communications to assist law enforcement.

As interception by government agents of communications between citizens is one of the more extreme manifestations of state power, those governments with a modicum of respect for the rule of law have at least shown some deference to human rights. In general, the more private the communication, the more exacting the procedural requirements for its interception. In common law countries, surveillance of public places can be done as a matter of routine. Access to stored communications data (voicemail or archived email) is also easily obtained, subject to subpoenas served on third parties, or ordinary search warrants served on the premises where the data are held. By contrast, telecommunications interception (that is, interception of communications during the course of transmission) may only be undertaken subject to the most exacting guidelines, requiring prior approval by an independent judicial authority. In practice, however, some countries have been known to pay mere lip service to these requirements (Risen and Lichtblau, 2005).

All of this and more characterize counter-terrorism strategies. Surveillance at most airports in developed countries around the world combines a visible human presence in the form of security guards, uniformed police, and at times, military personnel. These may be accompanied by plainclothes counterparts. Video surveillance is ubiquitous. In addition, a variety of technologies including metal detectors, x-rays and magnetic imaging are employed to scrutinize passengers' personal effects.

Inhibiting movement – detention strategies

Two challenges that confront democratic societies in their operational response to terrorism are overreaction and mistake. Governments may respond to an incident with disproportionate force, and in so doing may alienate supporters. Indeed, terrorist organizations may in fact seek to provoke such overreaction for just that reason. Another risk is that of mistake, that of pursuing the wrong person. Some cases involve elements of each.

Box 5.1   Jean Charles de Menezes, Mohamed Haneef, and Maher Arar

Jean Charles de Menezes was a Brazilian national living in London and working as an electrician. On July 22, 2005, Metropolitan Police were searching for suspects involved in an attempted bombing on the previous day. An address found with an unexploded bomb led them to an apartment

(Continued)

(Continued)

block where Menezes happened to be living. Menezes, who worked as an electrician, left his residence and boarded a bus and the London Underground en route to a job. Police followed him, assuming him to be one of the suspected bombers. Menezes was carrying a bag, thought by police to contain a bomb. Menezes was shot seven times in the head at point-blank range. http://www.ipcc.gov.uk/stockwell_one.pdf

Mohamed Haneef was an Indian doctor working in Australia in 2007. The year before, he spent time in England where he had visited two distant cousins. Prior to his departure from England, Dr Haneef left his telephone SIM card with one of them. A year later, a vehicle containing propane gas canisters was driven through glass doors at Glasgow International Airport and ignited. It was erroneously reported that the SIM card was found with one of the participants in the Glasgow attack, when it had been in the possession of a cousin in Liverpool. Authorities in Australia detained and eventually charged Dr Haneef, but were unable to obtain evidence that he was aware of any militant tendencies on the part of his cousin when he gave him the SIM card. Charges were eventually dropped. http://www.haneefcaseinquiry.gov.au/www/inquiry/haneefcaseinquiry.nsf/Page/Report

Maher Arar, an engineer with dual Canadian/Syrian citizenship, was arrested in the United States under suspicion of being a member of Al Qaeda. He had previously been seen by Canadian authorities in the company of a person of interest to a terrorism investigation. Arar was detained in the United States, and then deported to Syria where he claims to have been tortured during detention. After nearly a year he was released to Canada where an inquiry cleared him of any links to terrorism and where he was given a C$10.5 million settlement. The Commissioner of the Royal Canadian Mounted Police resigned after giving conflicting testimony about the case to a Parliamentary Committee. Arar is challenging his rendition in US courts, and he has never been charged by US authorities.http://www.sirc-csars.gc.ca/pdfs/cm_arar_rec-eng.pdf

Basic policy framework

The conventional response to organized crime in most English speaking democracies has involved an array of complementary legislative provisions. The first is a substantive criminal law that prohibits the kinds of activities that criminal organizations tend to engage in – extortion, murder, and the provision of a variety of illicit goods and services. The next is a set of criminal procedure laws that specify powers of search and seizure. As we have seen, the profit motive might not be the only motive for organized crime, but it is certainly important. For this reason, governments have developed two complementary strategies that target the assets of criminals, and the proceeds of crime. The third is a set of legislation specifically targeted at terrorism. We will explore each of these in turn.

Specific legislation

Schloenhardt (2009) developed a four-fold categorization of organized crime legislation. They are not mutually exclusive. The conspiracy model, based on English common law, contains special provisions that create criminal liability for conspiracies. It is common to jurisdictions in the English legal tradition, including the United States, Canada, Australia and New Zealand.

The *participation model*, with roots in continental Europe, is based on the two elements of *participation* in a *criminal organization*. This model had been adopted in a number of common law jurisdictions. Definitions of the two elements vary significantly from jurisdiction to jurisdiction; in some, participation must entail an overt act; in others, mere membership or physical presence may suffice.

The *enterprise model* is embodied in arguably the most prominent piece of legislation aimed specifically at organized crime: the (US) Racketeer Influenced and Corrupt Organizations (RICO) Act. Enacted in 1970, RICO provides for enhanced penalties for specified serious crimes committed by individuals involved in an ongoing criminal organization, as reflected in repeated criminal activity. RICO also contains provisions for civil lawsuits, where a private individual who has been harmed as a result of racketeering activity may recover treble damages from the defendant. RICO-type legislation has not been widely adopted outside the United States, presumably because other jurisdictions have fewer inhibitions about criminalizing membership in an organization, and find the other models more compatible with their legal cultures.

Schloenhardt's fourth category is the *labelling/registration model*. This covers the prohibition of certain organizations, making it an offence to associate with those organizations. Two Australian state jurisdictions have adopted this model in response to apparent heightened activity by outlaw motorcycle gangs. The model is also common to former British colonies such as Hong Kong, Singapore, and Malaysia.

Japan enacted anti-Yakuza legislation in 1992. Under that law, police are empowered to declare a business to be gang controlled, and thereby prohibit members from engaging with enterprises in certain industries. Japan has also established regional centers for promoting the eradication of Yakuza. Activities at these centres promote public awareness campaigns, assistance for members of the public to resist extortion demands, and the encouragement of defections from Yakuza gangs.

Japanese law also imposes vicarious liability on gang leaders for losses arising from offences committed by subordinate gang members.

Institutions may also be established by statute with the explicit purpose of targeting organized crime. The United Kingdom enacted the Serious Organised Crime and Police Act in 2005 which established the Serious Organized Crime Agency (SOCA). SOCA has both intelligence and law enforcement powers, which are shared with the 44 local police agencies. An interesting aspect of SOCA's activities are what it refers to as its 'harm reduction responsibilities.' In other words, it does not limit itself to post-hoc investigation of crimes that have been committed, but also extends to activities 'upstream.' SOCA claims not to pre-empt the conventional police forces of the UK but rather to assist them.

Responsibility for organized crime in Australia's federal system is shared between a number of national and state agencies. The Australian Federal Police bear responsibility for enforcing Commonwealth (i.e. federal) law. Each of the six states and two territories has its own criminal law, and its own police agency. Although jurisdiction may overlap in some cases (importing illicit substances is a federal offence, whereas possessing them is embraced by state law) there is a workable division of labor. To facilitate cooperation, an Australian Crime Commission was created with responsibility for coordinating multijurisdictional investigations of 'nationally significant' crime. Like SOCA in the UK, it has both intelligence and investigative responsibilities. Its legal foundation, including definitions of serious and organized crime, is the Australian Crime Commission Act 2002.

Cash transactions reporting

Those criminals who succeed in amassing significant ill-gotten gains are faced with the problem of concealing the source, lest they indicate to the state what they have been up to, and/or reveal evidence of the crimes they have committed. (Criminals also have an interest in concealing illicit income from taxation authorities; recall the misfortunes of Al Capone who was finally prosecuted successfully for income tax evasion rather than his violent felonies.) The practice of concealing the origins of 'dirty' money is colloquially referred to as 'money laundering.' This entails transferring the proceeds of crime from one place to another, then converting the wealth to a form that makes its origins untraceable or apparently legitimate. Thus governments focus on cash transactions reporting. This tends to involve systematic monitoring of financial transactions, usually by specialized agencies. Basically, banks or other defined cash dealers (these may be defined by law to include gold dealers, yacht brokers, etc.) are required by law to report transactions over a specific threshold (usually $US10,000 or lesser transactions of a suspicious nature) to the agency. Anti-money laundering policies have been implemented in many countries around the world, specifically in those with advanced economies. The policies have entailed the creation of a special agency, or a special division of an existing agency, to monitor the volume and pattern of financial transactions. In the United States, the agency in question resides within the Treasury Department and is called the Financial Crimes Enforcement Network (FinCEN). The Australian counterpart is the Australian Transaction Reports and Analysis Centre, or AUSTRAC.

Following the 9/11 attacks, governments became attentive to the fact that the financing of terrorist operations can also entail the movement of funds between financial institutions and across national borders. The challenge of interdicting such movement in the first place, or identifying the originator and ultimate recipient of these funds, is now part of the core business of cash transaction reporting agencies. One of the problems they confront, however, is the fact that terrorist operations often require very little in the way of cash, and alternative remittance systems exist such as hawala, which is dependent upon a system of trusted relationships or 'informal banks' that may defy monitoring by government authorities.

Confiscation of criminal assets

Governments also pursue strategies for the confiscation of the proceeds of crime. This can mean 'freezing' the assets pending determination of their illegitimate provenance, and then seizing them, either after a criminal conviction or (depending on the jurisdiction) pursuant to civil proceedings. Typical of such legislation is Australia's Proceeds of Crime Act 2002.

Confiscation of criminal assets may involve considerable challenges for the government. The logistics of disposal may be cumbersome and disposal may take some time to accomplish. At the same time, the government seeks to realize the best price for the goods in question. Certain kinds of property require considerable upkeep, which may be costly such as, for example, a luxury yacht or a stable of racehorses in training. Some years ago, one of the authors heard an anecdote relating to the seizure of a brothel. Even though this occurred in a jurisdiction where the sex industry was legal and regulated, it may have struck some as unseemly for the state to own a business of that nature.

Of course, organized criminals who anticipate government efforts to confiscate their ill-gotten gains may go to great lengths to conceal their assets and obscure their beneficial ownership. This too, may pose formidable challenges for the government. Among these is the risk to innocent third parties. In those jurisdictions which are empowered to confiscate property used in the production or transport of drugs, one has seen the seizure of homes belonging to unwitting landlords, or yachts owned by leasers who were quite unaware of the use to which their property had been put (Ayling et al., 2009).

Legislating against terrorism

The events of September 11, 2001 instigated a flurry of legislative activity around the world. Most prominent among this was the USA PATRIOT Act (an acronym for, 'Uniting and Strengthening America by Providing Appropriate Tools Required to Intercept and Obstruct Terrorism'). The Act, which became law on 26 October 2001 is a wide-ranging statute that increased powers of surveillance (roving wiretaps; email intercepts), search and seizure of evidence (so called 'sneak and peek' warrants), and detention of terrorist suspects. It also provides for enhanced border security and strengthened anti-money laundering provisions in order to inhibit the financing of terrorist activities.

Box 5.2   USA PATRIOT Act

The Uniting and Strengthening America by Providing Appropriate Tools Required to Intercept and Obstruct Terrorism Act of 2001 (USA PATRIOT Act) was signed into law on 26 October 2001. Instigated by the attacks of September 11, the Act contained a variety of provisions including:

- A broader definition of terrorism;
- Increased powers to intercept telecommunications;
- Increased penalties for those convicted of terrorism offences;
- Increased powers to collect intelligence on terrorism and related activity;
- Enhanced border security;
- Additional financial reporting and record keeping requirements to discourage terrorist financing;
- It also provided for assistance to families of victims of terrorist acts.

In addition, Sec. 813 of the PATRIOT Act defined terrorism as racketeering activity, bringing it under the ambit of the Racketeer Influenced and Corrupt Organizations Act for good measure.

The heavy handed response of the Bush administration to the issue of terrorism proved to be costly indeed. Ironically, the administration went to great lengths to maintain the appearance of legality. This led to the practice of transporting terrorist suspects to nations willing to provide facilities and skills to be used in aggressive interrogation of suspects. When these renditions became public knowledge, they did little to uphold the image of the United States as the 'leader of the free world' or as the 'beacon of democracy.'

It is not always apparent whether a given criminal act (such as ATM fraud or smuggling cash) is related to a terrorist conspiracy. It may not be surprising therefore to learn that the USA PATRIOT Act has been used in a wide spectrum of cases beyond terrorism (Lichtblau, 2005). Critics, of course, would argue that legislation which represents an overreaction to terrorism is even less appropriate to apply to ordinary crime.

Witness protection

As we have seen, exiting from a criminal organization or terrorist group can be difficult and dangerous. The danger may become even more acute if the defector in question is prepared to turn against his former colleagues and to assist the government in investigation and prosecution. In recent years, governments have sought to facilitate defection from criminal organizations by establishing witness protection programs. In return for their cooperation, defectors (and their families) may be offered a new identity, employment, and relocation, as well as close personal protection (bodyguards) in extreme cases.

Complementary regulatory interventions

Neither organized crime nor terrorism exists in a vacuum. Individuals or organizations of either stripe often have dealings with a variety of legitimate (and often unwitting) institutions. The creation of an unfavorable environment for illicit organizations often means harnessing the resources and energies of individuals and institutions outside the criminal justice or national security systems.

Standard anti-money laundering programs rely on financial institutions to detect and disclose suspicious transactions. In their discussion of organized crime in New York City, Jacobs et al. (1999) relate how the creation of licensing regimes made it more difficult for criminal organizations to exploit wholesale fish markets and waste haulage industries.

Airlines have an obligation to enforce immigration laws by checking the validity of travellers' documentation (Gilboy, 1998). Large fines against airlines may be imposed if they fail to check properly the validity of passports and visas to the countries to which they are delivering passengers. In the United States, commercial carriers are required to use due diligence to prevent the use of their conveyance for the importation of illegal drugs.

The advent of privatization in most western industrial societies has meant that most critical infrastructure – transport, communications, finance, utilities, and the like, is now privately owned. The increased threat of terrorism has moved governments to influence or compel private owners of infrastructure to safeguard their assets from terrorist attack.

Disruption

One strategy for combating illicit organizations might be described as disruption – that is, harassment of the organization and its members in a manner that creates a hostile environment for their activities. As such, it is a strategy of prevention, or pre-emption, as opposed to a reactive strategy of pursuing offenders after the offence has been committed.

This is a basic strategy of the Serious Organized Crime Agency (SOCA) in the UK and has been practiced by the US Federal Bureau of Investigation for the better part of half a century.

Harassment of organizations deemed to be illicit may also entail fairly draconian methods. Disruption can involve, inter alia, extensive surveillance, both visual and electronic; measures to foment discord within the target organization; and the use of lesser legislative or regulatory tools to make organizational life difficult. Prominent organized crime figure Sam Giancana was subjected to relentless and intensive surveillance by the FBI during the 1960s. One Chicago mobster was charged and convicted for offences relating to possession of mourning doves (Kaiser, 2008: 85).

The efforts of the FBI to discredit Martin Luther King, Jr. are among the more vivid examples of harassment. These entailed extensive electronic surveillance, disclosure of King's extramarital affairs to his wife, and the sending of anonymous death threats to King himself (Garrow, 1981). This is not to suggest that King was either a criminal or a suspected terrorist. Rather, his campaign for racial equality was perceived as threatening by the US elites of the 1960s and particularly by J. Edgar Hoover, the director of the Federal Bureau of Investigation, who directed much of the surveillance.

Illicit organizations, like organizations generally, are vulnerable to factionalism and discord. Law enforcement and intelligence agencies may exploit these vulnerabilities by creating or aggravating these internal divisions in a target group.

Whether they occur spontaneously or with a little help from the state, conflicts within and between illicit organizations may evolve in unpredictable ways. So-called gangland wars may escalate dramatically. In extreme circumstances, innocent third parties may become literally or figuratively caught in the crossfire. A spate of highly publicized murders, even when the victims themselves are criminals, can be unsettling to the law abiding public, and may create the impression that the state is incapable of controlling organized crime.

The use of tax law to bring about the demise of Al Capone is part of American organized crime legend. This served as the model for subsequent anti-organized crime strategies in the United States. The Kennedy Administration's efforts to contain the Mafia were based in part on the use of tax and other administrative laws to target key subjects.

At times, state response to both terrorism and organized crime can be extremely aggressive. States themselves may borrow a page from the books of their adversaries, although they usually seek to conceal circumstances where they themselves break the law.

Successful pursuits of suspected organized criminals do not always result in surrender. In some cases, the target will resist apprehension, and seek to flee or to defend him or herself. The legal circumstances of such confrontations are not always clear cut. One might envisage a continuum ranging from lawful arrest without violence at one extreme, to cold-blooded assassination of an offender at the other. As observed in the Introduction, the summary execution of suspected organized criminals in India is sufficiently common that the practice is euphemistically referred to as an 'encounter.'

The role of the media in fostering a climate of fear

The media in contemporary society perform a number of functions. Among the most important of these, especially in democratic societies, is to inform the citizenry on matters of public policy. As most media are commercial enterprises, another important objective is to make money for their proprietors. Related to their commercial function is that of entertaining their audience. Boring news programs, no less than boring fiction, attract fewer readers, listeners, or viewers. As circulations decline, so too do profits.

Most people also like to think of themselves as virtuous, or at least, not malevolent. For centuries now, literature and legend have juxtaposed good and evil. To some extent, contemporary news media perform the function of medieval morality plays, allowing the public to identify with the 'good guys' and to distance themselves from the 'forces of evil.' A public seeking simplicity and certainty is often uncomfortable with moral ambiguity. This is somewhat problematic in a world where there are many gray areas. Those who may not be attracted to 'horror movies' will at least acknowledge their commercial profitability. And so it is that the media, wittingly or otherwise, may at times accentuate the gruesome.

What all this means is that news coverage of terrorism and counter-terrorism is often something other than balanced, rational reportage. Bennett et al. (2007) have argued that media coverage in the west tends to have a built in authority bias because of journalistic conventions which seek 'official' comments which often provide the lead and 'frame' (narrative structure) for the story. When governments have a vested interest in advancing a certain interpretation of events or individuals, the potential for distortion becomes even greater.

Another characteristic of wartime is the practice of 'demonizing' the enemy. A state may portray the enemy as evil incarnate for two basic purposes. First, by invoking the spectre of an evil threat, a state may attempt to engender social solidarity among its own citizens. Second, the image of evil may be used to justify extraordinary action against 'the other' and to help reduce inhibitions on the part of those who might be called upon to take such action. Extraordinary efforts to dehumanize the enemy were made by both Japanese and United States governments during World War II (Dower, 1986). Readers will note that such demonization is hardly the monopoly of states, and may also characterize the perspective of terrorists and of organized criminals. The utter ruthlessness with which the 9/11 hijackers targeted civilian populations, and with which the assassins of judges Falcone and Borsellino detonated immense explosions in furtherance of the murders, is illustrative.

Demonization is but one extreme of a wider strategy that one might refer to as delegitimation. Terrorists and organized criminals exist in wider communities. The extent to which members of these communities are supportive (or at least tolerant) of the illicit organization and its activities can be crucial to the organization's sustainability. Efforts to discredit or to disparage the illicit organization and its members can take many forms.

Ironically, some of the most effective delegitimation of illicit organizations is achieved by the organizations themselves. The erosion of support for Al Qaeda in much of the Muslim world has been attributed to their indiscriminate violence against other Muslims. The assassinations of judges Falcone and Borsellino brought hundreds of thousands of Italians into the streets to express their indignation over Mafia brutality (Cowell, 1992).

Box 5.3   Giovanni Falcone and Paolo Borsellino

Giovanni Falcone and Paolo Borsellino were magistrates in Palermo, Italy, who specialized in the investigation of mafia activities (in the Italian legal system, judicial officers play an active role in criminal investigation). The two contributed to the conviction of hundreds of members of the Sicilian mafia during the 1980s, including the celebrated 'Maxi-Trial.'

On May 23, 1992 Falcone, his wife, and three bodyguards were killed by a 350kg roadside bomb which was detonated as their car was travelling from Palermo Airport into the city. Less than two months later, on July 19, 1992 Borsellino and five police officers were killed by a bomb as he was on his way to visit his mother in Palermo.

Following the Falcone and Borsellino assassinations, protests against mafia activity and in support of increased police powers occurred throughout Italy. Palermo's airport is named in their honour. (Paoli, 2003: 204)

Rehabilitation

In some cases, it may be possible to assist former members of illicit organizations to reject their past and be reintegrated into society. For those who may be resented and perhaps even targeted by their former colleagues, we have discussed witness protection programs. In other circumstances, re-education and rehabilitation programs may be appropriate. The nature and circumstances of such programs will vary, depending upon the backgrounds of the individuals in question and the host cultures of those states who establish the program. Among the more prominent are those programs developed in Saudi Arabia and Indonesia for the reintegration of those who have previously embraced some of the more militant forms of Islam. The Saudi counseling program combines religious instruction with psychological counseling, and a variety of benefits including health care, income support, and assistance in finding employment. Saudi authorities are reported to have claimed at least an 80 percent success rate (Boucek, 2009; Zoepf, 2008). Nevertheless, there have been cases of relapse (Worth, 2009a, 2009b; Pluchinsky, 2008) and the long-term success rate of the program is still in doubt.

SIX

conclusions: managing crime and terrorism

In this chapter we explore the factors contributing to the decline of terrorist and criminal organizations. We focus upon both the organizational dynamics that may contribute to such declines, and the factors contributing to the decisions by individual members of criminal and terrorist organizations to leave these organizations. As we shall see, the web of relationships which connect these communities, the state, and illicit organizations may significantly impact on these decisions. It is thus important to consider opportunities for interdicting both terrorist and criminal organizations by weakening their support within the community and by encouraging the consideration of 'leaving terrorism and criminality behind' (see Bjørgo and Horgan, 2009).

To understand the decline of illicit organizations it is useful to remember that the frameworks presented in earlier chapters which discussed both the genesis and development of illicit organizations, and the recruitment and sustaining of individual membership will assist in understanding the decline of illicit organizations, the disengagement from these organizations and the desistance of activity of individual members.

The Demise of Illicit Organizations

How terrorism ends

While the reading of our daily newspaper might not present this impression, eventually, most terrorist groups (and most individual terrorists) stop what they are doing. In rare cases, they stop because many of the goals for which they organized to pursue have been attained (most often in the context of a much wider political movement). The African National Congress became the governing political party in a democratic South Africa. On the eve of their victory over the British, which led to the founding of the State of Israel, Irgun was dismantled by the other Jewish political organizations because it was judged to threaten that victory. Almost 30 years later in 1977 its last leader, Menachem Begin, became Prime Minister. The FLN (the National Liberation Front) prevailed over French colonial forces and brought about the independence of Algeria in 1962. In addition, some terrorist groups that have not secured a definitive triumph have obtained a seat at the 'bargaining table,' as did the IRA after the Good Friday Agreement, 1998.

In fact, most terrorist groups stop because they fail, some sooner than others and far sooner than our common impressions. According to Rapoport (1992) only 10 percent survive as long as one year, less than five percent as long as a decade. The demise of a terrorist organization may be the result of internal or external factors or both. Internally, terrorist groups may founder because of strategic miscalculation or internal dissention. Or, they may fail because of the loss of a leader, and the lack of processes for leadership succession. Their priorities may also evolve so that they turn to crime. Externally, they may be defeated by a state, a competing group or they may lose their base of internal or external support or the acquiescence of the society within which they operate.

The demise of criminal organizations

Likewise, conventional criminal organizations rarely go on forever. The factors contributing to their demise are quite similar to those of terrorist organizations. In some cases, they are simply 'outgunned' (literally or figuratively) by the state. Almost the entire membership of the five Hell's Angels chapters in the Canadian province of Quebec was arrested in April, 2009.

Rather unlike terrorist organizations however, conventional criminal groups may have competition. This often involves aggressive efforts to maintain 'market share.' So called 'gang wars' occasionally break out in 'tit for tat' assassinations.

But it is also important to recognize that there are some criminal organizations that, because of their historical development, are more tightly woven into the fabric of society, even if that wider society no longer values or supports their existence. These organizations developed in a particular historical period to challenge the state and, in part, to defend the local communities from coercive extraction. The Mafia are a prime example (Blok, 1975). The Yakuza often proclaim themselves to be the descendents of the machi-yokko (servants of the town) who protected their villages from the wayward hatamoto-yakko (Kaplan and Dubro, 2003). The Triads had their origin in anti-Manchu resistance in China (Ownby, 2001).

On the interdiction of terrorist and criminal organizations

Organizational decline may occur naturally. As indicated above, it may occur when a terrorist organization loses its raison d'être for employing terror, such as when some of its organizational objectives are achieved. For example, when there is a transition to a legitimate political process for terrorist groups – 'a place at the table.' Interestingly, the natural decline may also be accelerated by the willingness of the leadership of such groups to enter the 'legitimate' political arena and begin talks as happened in the case of Fatah, which after more than 30 years chose to begin the process of negotiation with the Israelis. While the organization still exists, it has lost its base and support in Gaza, ironically creating a problem for both the organization and its Israeli government counterpart. While rarer, this may also occur when external enemies or threats disappear or are mitigated, such as what happens when occupying forces withdraw or changes in state regimes occur. Similarly, Bjørgo (1999) argues that in the case of gangs which have developed as protection against other gangs perceived as threats, if the counter gang disappears and the threat comes to an end, the raison d'être for the gang disappears and the organization declines or evolves into another form.

Cronin (2009: 97), using examples of failures of the Red Brigade, the Red Army Faction and other left wing groups of the 1970s, argues that natural decline may also be due to an unsuccessful generational transition caused by the inability of ideological groups to maintain or pass on the ideology to a successor generation. These groups, which had formed because of a particular, time-based interpretation of their contemporary situation, thus found it difficult to generate sufficient numbers of new recruits or maintain organizational relevance for the next 'generation' of members. (Ironically at the same time as this failure, leaders of NATO nations, a major focus of the European left wing groups, were also concerned about developing continuing support for NATO amongst the next generation of NATO country leaders. See Szabo, 1984). Recruitment into the organization was based on 'like mindedness,' a common intellectual interpretation of wrongs that needed to be redressed. These types of organizations are much more difficult to maintain than those based on shared identities and social ties built upon firm social foundations, which helps explain the easier organizational recruitment for ethno-nationalist movements. It also helps explain their ability to maintain themselves from generation to generation as long as the political raison d'être continues to exist. Thus, the terrorist movements that have shown decline (and in many cases simply disappearance) over the past 30 years have been the ideologically based movements such as the RAF, Action Directe, and Red Brigades of Germany, France, and Italy, respectively, whereas those that have shown the greatest resilience have been the ethno-nationalist movements such as the ETA (Basque Fatherland and Liberty), the Sri Lankan-based Liberation Tigers of Tamil Eelam, the IRA, and the numerous Palestinian groups.

This history also helps to explain the message of organizations such as Al Qaeda. which is often simply viewed through the lens of Islamic fundamentalism by western governments and publics. In their attempt to forestall organizational decline which might occur if they simply had a 'narrow' religious message, Al Qaeda consistently employs a recruiting message which is based on the continued occupation by outsiders (i.e. non Muslims) of lands (e.g. Israel) that should be controlled by Muslims. They also condemn the control of lands by apostate regimes such as Saudi Arabia, Kuwait, and Algeria.

Clearly then, organizational decline can be hastened or encouraged by external forces which stem the flow of new recruits to the organization.

Organizations work hard to encourage their continuing renewal, particularly when they are actively engaged in a struggle in which they are constantly losing members. New recruitment can be inhibited by authorities, both local and international, through pre-emption and deterrence strategies. Ross and Gurr (1989) discuss four general kinds of conditions which can contribute to the decline of political terrorism: preemption, deterrence, burnout and backlash (discussed below), which may also usefully be considered with respect to criminals and criminal organizations. *Pre-emption* and *deterrence* are counterterrorist and law enforcement policies and actions which can reduce or eliminate the terrorists' coercive capabilities and the opportunities and options of criminals. Pre-emptive and deterrence strategies increase the risks of engaging in illicit activities for both individuals and organizations and often serve to reduce the capacity to move persons, information and materials freely and unnoticed within societies. These strategies include increasing surveillance capabilities and activities, inhibiting movement across borders by tightening up immigration controls and increasing customs checks, establishing checkpoints and traffic stops, examining cargo and increasing the regulation and monitoring of goods, services, and financial flows (including bank accounts, tax filings and investments), pressuring sponsors (known and suspected) and penalizing collaborators, rewarding turncoats and targeting safe havens both internal and external to the group's current location. Each of the strategies can of course be countered by changing modes of operation, shifting patterns of movement, altering destinations and points of access. If these adaptive measures are well designed and well implemented, and the targeted organization invests new time and resources to do so, changes will be possible. But adaptation will come at a price to the organization; those investments will increase its costs and, at least in the short term, reduce its capabilities.

Of course, states also pursue strategies, beyond the disruption of the capacities of organization, which aim at destroying the organization itself. A very frequent choice is to engage in a strategy of decapitation, cutting off the top of the organization. Thus states target the organization's senior leadership. From a public perspective this appears a logical, common sense approach, as many of these criminal and terrorist organizations are presented in terms of their leadership and the organization is personified by the leader that the public has come to fear or hate. In the past 40 years, a number of terrorist and criminal organization 'stars' have dominated the public image of these illicit organizations, e.g. Carlos the Jackal, Osama bin Laden, Abu Musab al-Zarqawi, John Gotti, Salvatore Riina, and Bernardo Provenzano. Of these, all but Osama bin Laden are imprisoned or deceased, yet the organizations which they led or 'represented' all continue to exist and pursue their ends. In the criminal realm, this often leads to police and prosecutorial strategies which build interdiction and adjudication cases from below, sacrificing short term arrest, crime cessation and convictions of lower level organization members in pursuit of the next person up the organizational hierarchy in search of major disruptions to the organization. The focus becomes the leadership and many of the organizational processes thus remain in place as the targets move up the organizational hierarchy.

This may be a double-edged sword. There is no question that the public who support the government are a significant part of the audience for actions against organized crime and terrorism. They wish to see action against the organizations that are carrying out terrorist acts or committing crime. If the counterterrorism or crime control policy is described as centering on elimination of the leader, and the leader is not apprehended or convicted of the crimes with which they are charged, the public's trust in government and/or their faith in that government declines. Witness the cynicism resulting from identifying the US War on Terror in terms of George Bush's campaign against Osama bin Laden and Al Qaeda. Despite the elimination of many key members of the Al Qaeda hierarchy, and numerous claims of eliminating Al Qaeda's number two member in this or that hierarchy, the public continued to believe that the approach was not successful. This perception also derived from an additional tactical mistake on the part of the Bush administration. In battling for the hearts and minds of the public, it is important that states take care to avoid inflated rhetoric that makes the problem of crime and terrorism worse than it actually is. The Al Qaeda attack on September 11, 2001 was a horrendous crime and signified the destruction that could be caused by the organization. However, the organization did not threaten the existence of the United States, and raising the response to the level of war dramatically increased expectations about the resources and capabilities of both Al Qaeda's threat and the level of the US response. With the passage of time and lack of resolution on the problem of bin Laden and Al Qaeda, consider the statements of Mr Bush less than a year later, in March 2002:

> Well, as I say, we haven't heard much from him. And I wouldn't necessarily say he's at the center of any command structure. And, again, I don't know where he is. I – I'll repeat what I said. I truly am not that concerned about him. I know he is on the run. I was concerned about him, when he had taken over a country. I was concerned about the fact that he was basically running Afghanistan and calling the shots for the Taliban.

> But once we set out the policy and started executing the plan, he became – we shoved him out more and more on the margins. He has no place to train his Al Qaeda killers anymore. And if we – excuse me for a minute – and if we find a training camp, we'll take care of it. Either we will or our friends will. That's one of the things – part of the new phase that's becoming apparent to the American people is that we're working closely with other governments to deny sanctuary, or training, or a place to hide, or a place to raise money.

One consequence of what is therefore perceived as not only failure to carry out the state's objectives but 'hype' is to increase public cynicism, even to the point that governments are accused of attempting to score political points and manipulate the public rather than addressing the root causes of the problem.

In addition it is important to recognize that any official statements that may serve to elevate the status of an adversary to justify the need for either swift or escalated action, whether that adversary is a terrorist group or an outlaw motorcycle gang, may create difficulties in managing responses and expectations. The state should not serve, wittingly or otherwise, to increase the glamour of gangster chic. Stern (2006) argues that 'jihad' has become a fad for many Muslim youth today, just as revolution was for young people all over the world in the 1960s. Similarly, the use of such military metaphors as 'the war on terror' elevates the terrorist's status to that of combatant. Simply labeling terrorists as common criminals may be preferable.

On the other hand, there have been significant government successes, as other illicit organizations and leaders have not fared as well and have succumbed to government forces. Organizations whose leaders are especially charismatic, and not simply a public face of the organization, may be particularly vulnerable when the leader in question is captured or killed. This is particularly likely to be the case if the leader has not translated his charisma into a viable organizational structure independent of the charisma. Following the 1995 arrest of Shoko Asahara, leader of Aum Shinrikyo, the group's membership declined by 90 percent. The capture of Abimael Guzman of Peru's Shining Path led to an even greater drop. The arrest of Abdullah Ocalan, leader of the Kurdistan Worker's Party, severely weakened the organization politically, leading some members to abandon political struggle and turn their attentions to conventional criminality. Other examples of 'fighters turned felons' include Abu Sayyaf in the Philippines and various narco-terrorist groups in Colombia.

Success in eliminating leaders of such organizations is often greeted with much applause but it is also greeted with the expectation that once the leader is gone, the terrorism will subside or the crime will diminish. In the three cases above this was indeed the case. But it has also been the case, as with Zarqawi in Iraq, the continuing Israeli success in targeting key members of the enemy with assassination, and the consistent success of the British government in incarcerating key members of the Irish Republican Army, that the terrorism continues and the terrorist organizations continue to function. Likewise, prosecutorial success over the past 50 years in the United States against various Mafia crime bosses has not meant the end of the organization, or the organized crime problem in general. This is illustrated by the case of John Gotti, head of the Gambino crime family, arguably the most important of the American crime families. When Gotti was convicted on Racketeering Influenced and Corrupt Organization (RICO) charges and sentenced to life in prison, his son became head of the crime family. The family, though further diminished by the testimony of one of its members turned informant, continued to operate. In December 2009 a federal judge declared a mistrial in the latest RICO trial against Gotti, Jr. It was the fourth time in five years that Gotti was able to avoid conviction.

These examples illustrate that the success of such a strategy is dependent upon more than the success of eliminating or incarcerating the organization's titular head or leadership. The structure of the targeted organization, the ability of members below the top echelon to move up and take over, and the methods and 'collateral damage' caused by the actions taken to decapitate also need to be considered. They may also indicate that capturing or imprisoning a leader will only be effective in causing organizational decline if the leader is unable to have further influence on organizational members (Cronin, 2006: 22). There is also the risk that decapitation of an organization by removal of a charismatic leader will create a martyr and thereby lead to an organizational renaissance, though this is much more likely in the case of ethno-nationalist struggles in which the leader has been able to tie him or herself to an important foundational myth or leader. For example, while the execution of Che Guevara created a martyr for an international audience whose image remains an icon more than four decades after his death, Guevara's death did not inspire a further uprising within Bolivia or resonate with the particular audience inside the country he was trying to lead to liberation. The bombing death of FRELIMO (Frente de Libertação de Moçambique) leader Eduardo Mondlane in 1969, most likely at the hands of the Portuguese government that he and his organization were fighting, served to inspire Mozambiquan resistance. Six years later Portugal handed over Mozambique to FRELIMO.

Which suppression tactic is most effective to hasten organizational decline will depend on the organization's structure. For instance, targeting leadership may be effective in dealing with a hierarchy but ineffective for a cellular structure, where targeting brokers – the connecting links between parts of the organization – may be more successful. Williams (2001: 93), in fact, argues that a strategy to target 'cut-points', i.e. those 'critical nodes' who are not necessarily leaders but constitute the main or sole link between different parts of the organization, is the most effective way to hasten organizational decline (see also McGloin, 2005: 626). It also appears that organizations which have a networked architecture are more resistant to state attempts at interdiction than those with a bureaucratic or hierarchical form (Kenney, 2007: 32). Because of the success of campaigns against them, some organizations attempt out of necessity to decentralize when under attack by law enforcement (Morselli, 2009). Ironically, some state success in strategies of decapitation against a criminal organization may be ineffective in the long term if the criminal organization adapts in a way that makes future state action against it more difficult (e.g. transforms from a hierarchy to a more decentralized network). That said, as with licit organizations, not all organizational adaptation under stress will be successful and the organization may not be as capable because operations or resource acquisition become more difficult.

Increasingly, states worry about the possibilities that terrorist and criminal organizations, under progressive organizational threat and with declining abilities to obtain the resources they need or safe havens within which to operate, will turn to one another for mutual support. This can mean mobilizing their support networks, markets, and capabilities as a way to overcome the increasing capacity of state coercive methods. While state concern is real, the point of intersection between terrorists and criminals may provide law enforcement with an important source of organizational leverage. Despite the fact that the criminal and terrorist organizations might have cause to collaborate, the differences in the organizational imperatives that created the two different forms of organization remain important, and the differences in the recruitment patterns and memberships create potential for exploiting mistrust and uncertainty.

As clandestine organizations threatened by local and international law enforcement, both forms of organization are constantly concerned about the security of their own networks. As indicated above, avoidance of discovery of their structure and dimensions remain paramount. Entrance into and departures from the organization are constant worries. It is at these entrance points that the organizations are likely to be most insecure. Organized criminal groups that have been long established in their home states and have developed within that state depend on existing institutional and financial structures to earn, maintain and protect their profits. In short they want predictability and want to know whom they can continue to bribe, corrupt and ensnare. They don't like change and they don't like organizations that may threaten that predictability. Increasing numbers of terrorist organizations are dependent on their own sources of income. Smaller cells may be cut off from more structured and resilient organizations. Organizations may follow the leaderless resistance model, in which groups emerge and organize without any central organizational direction beyond inspiration. Each of these changes may entail increasing numbers of amateurs and members who are cut off from organizational routines as well as resources. These smaller cells are therefore more reliant on their own resources and thus more likely to have to seek the cooperation of others to engage in crime to support themselves or to seek resources to accomplish their goals. These both increase the number of potential 'bad guys' and the number of intersections in which to catch them doing something to survive as an organization rather than as failed terrorists. Greater opportunities for infiltration into both terrorist and criminal networks arise and greatly increase the chances of detection of the smaller, amateur cells if they need to discover paths to criminal networks. Such was the case with the arrest in June 2006 of seven men allegedly plotting to blow up the Sears Tower in Chicago. The seven wanted to align themselves with Al Qaeda and as it transpired, engaged an FBI informant to secure weapons for them. After three trials, five of the seven were found guilty of the plot. Catching the disconnected amateurs is not likely to lead to anyone further up the terrorist network because the amateurs themselves have no connections. When they do have connections, the individuals in either the terrorist organization or the criminal organization are more likely to protect their mates and give up the 'other' if confronted by a choice of which organization to protect should things go wrong.

Activities that erode community support for either terrorists or organized crime will greatly enhance the likelihood of successful interventions by the state. These include encouraging a backlash by seeking means to alienate the illicit organization from the community (Ross and Gurr, 1989). Accommodative political strategies initiated by governments as a response to terrorist threats or actions may also serve to reduce the acquiescence of societies to the terrorists in their midst if the organizational leaders do not respond positively and/or accept the gains offered by the authorities. Accommodative offers, as minimal as they may be, offer the hope of a continued presence on the political agenda. They force populations who are not directly linked to the organization (but whose support or acquiescence is vital to the organizations' survival) to consider whether continued adherence to the ultimate goals of the organization or continuing tolerance for the 'right to exist' is worth the everyday effects of the continued presence

of the terrorists. Such a rational calculus brought on by official governmental action is more likely to create a backlash from the wider society
undermining the political capabilities of doctrinal terrorist movements
than those of clan or ethno-nationalist organizations. Within such
a communicative context, it is easier for governmental actions to
isolate the organization. But it is also important that states recognize
the public's perception of the terrorist or criminal organization and its
historical embeddedness and symbolic meaning within the community
so as to avoid unnecessarily alienating the very public it is trying to
win over. Anthropologists Ann and Peter Schneider argue for example
how important it is within Sicily, even for those fighting the Mafia to
recognize:

> The dilemma experienced by the participants, who share both location
> and history with the mafia. Dedicated to the anti-mafia struggle, activists
> are also loyal to their Sicilian identity, and in some cases burdened by a
> past of ambiguous social relations with people close to mafiosi. The result-
> ing moral anguish has been even more troubling because 'Sicilians' are so
> often treated as a stigmatized category by the wider world. (Schneider and
> Schneider, 2002: 777)

Through strategic misjudgment or plain bad luck, both terrorist and
criminal organizations succeed now and then in creating a backlash
for themselves without the assistance of the state. To use a sporting
metaphor, they score 'own goals.' Such counterproductive criminal
activity can include gratuitous violence, or violence directed against
innocent civilians. The massive explosions that caused the deaths
of Italian magistrates Falcone and Borsellino constituted literal overkill.
Members of the Real Irish Republican Army detonated a bomb at
Omagh in 1998 which killed 20 adults and nine children. This
cost them dearly in terms of public support. The public reaction of
the Saudi people to the Al Qaeda bombings in Riyadh in May and
November 2003 created a new climate in which the regime could
begin to crack down on Islamic extremists – something they were
loathe to do as long as there was public sympathy for the terrorists.
'Most of the victims [of the bombings] were Arabs of modest means;
this sloppy targeting undoubtedly cost Al Qaeda some of its support
in the kingdom' (Pillar, 2004: 106). Interestingly, it would appear

that Al Qaeda's leadership, often thought of as simply interested in large numbers of deaths, 'learned' from its attack in Saudi Arabia. In addition to recognizing that it underestimated the Saudi government's response, it also took note of the Saudi public's support of the resultant crackdown. Evidence of this learning may be seen in the reaction of the leadership in the aftermath of the indiscriminate killing of Muslims by Al Qaeda in Iraq in 2005 that appeared to weaken Al Qaeda's local support. In July 2005, concerned that this was a likely outcome, Ayman al-Zawahiri, Al Qaeda's second in command, wrote to Abu Musab al-Zarqawi, the now deceased leader of Al Qaeda in Iraq, to chastise Zarqawi and ask him to refrain from such actions because the killing would separate the organization from the Muslim masses, concluding, 'The mujahed movement must avoid any action that the masses do not understand or approve, if there is no contravention of Sharia in such avoidance, and as long as there are other options to resort to…' (Zawahiri, 2005).

When organized criminals battle each other, they, too, exercise extreme care to avoid harm to innocent third parties. Even when targeting a victim, they understand the importance of not accidentally harming bystanders and those outside the boundaries of acceptability. For example, in the case of the Italian Mafia, wives and young children are outside the boundaries of enforcement. Should these principles be violated, there is a risk that public indignation may facilitate a forceful state response.

States, too, are capable of overkill. Indeed, sometimes this propensity is exploited by terrorist groups who seek to goad the state into alienating the wider community. One clear consequence was evident in the Bush administration's War on Terror, particularly extending the War on Terror from targeting Al Qaeda and its Taliban hosts in Afghanistan to attacking Iraq under the mistaken arguments of links with Al Qaeda and the existence of weapons of mass destruction that could be shared with it. This led to the clear judgment of a significant portion of the population of the Muslim (as well as non-Muslim) world that the United States had exceeded acceptable limits of response. The result was a rapid decline in support for the United States and reluctance on the part of many populations and their governments to support United States counter terror efforts.

At a much smaller death level but with very large and long lasting consequences for the British state, consider the actions of January 30,

1972 in Derry (or Londonderry as it is was then named by the British state). Thirteen Irish Catholics lost their lives as 27 protestors were shot by British paratroopers during a march sponsored by the Northern Irish Civil Rights Association. This event, labeled Bloody Sunday, became a symbol of the overreaction and intransigence of the British state and the Northern Ireland protestant establishment. It was directly responsible for the hardening of the Catholic public's demands, as well as the significant boost in support for and recruitment into the Irish Republican Army.

Individual desistance and disengagement

Another means of countering terrorist and criminal organizations is to target the organizational membership itself. All organizations are dependent upon a steady flow of new recruits to do the work of the organization. In illicit organizations, the state attempts to stem the flow of recruits to reduce the capacity of the organization to conduct its operations. The state also seeks to disengage members from the organization through the death or apprehension, prosecution and incarceration of the organization. We may describe this in terms of involuntary disengagement or desistance from the organization. It is not only the state that may seek involuntary disengagement. The illicit organization may also end membership. Some members may be expelled from illicit organizations because they engage in activity that brings unwanted attention to the group or because they engaged in activities that were expressly forbidden by the group. Others may be expelled because they engaged in 'criminal' activities against the interests of the group, embezzling or diverting funds, freelancing, or challenging the authority of the leader or the decision making of the group and thereby threatening the security or cohesion of the organization. Because of the risk that a former member, following expulsion, may be persuaded to inform on his or her former colleagues, it is not unusual that expulsion is accompanied by execution. More charitable punishment might be severe beatings.

This is an ongoing and obvious struggle between authorities and illicit organizations. Beside the constant stress of potential discovery and apprehension, there are also voluntary departures of members created because these members have decided they no longer wish to be part of the group. Often this is described in terms of the member's *burnout*. Burnout may be linked to operational failures, political failures, increased stress caused by successes against the organization, and apprehension of other members by the state. It may be accompanied by disillusionment. The idealism which attracts people to terrorist groups, and the romance of or at least the dream of riches that may be garnered through attachment to a criminal organization, may become tarnished by the often grim reality of the dirty work and the rather poor rewards or the belief that the rewards (political or pecuniary) are never likely to materialize. Disillusionment may arise because of deaths of fellow members, disappointments in organizational activities and lack of success. It may also flow from collateral damage – the deaths of innocents in operations in which either the individual or the organization was involved or as retaliation for activities undertaken, or anger at the inability of the organization or its leadership to accomplish its goals. The disillusionment may be more likely when the member believes that the work and the reward are inequitably distributed within the organization and when the reward/ risk ratio appears to be highly skewed toward the risk side of the balance. When idealism turns to cynicism in the case of terrorist groups, or optimism to pessimism in criminal groups as to the future of rewards in material or organizational terms, interpersonal conflict within the organization may arise. Differences of opinion may occur over tactics, or broader strategic issues may become more vocal and pronounced.

The disillusionment may be accompanied or exacerbated by psychological disengagement because of changes in priorities connected to the aging process (marriage, children, and deaths of family members and/ or aging itself). In all militant organizations, licit and illicit, the aging of members is accompanied by burnout. When organizational life is continuously stressful, and hope is not reinforced by victories or riches, older members may simply weary of the struggle, and opt out.

With reference to terrorist organizations, it is important to remember that the greatest numbers are recruited in their teens and twenties and begin departing in their thirties as they lose hope in 'making a difference' and seek to 'live their life' (see Russell and Miller, 1977: 18; Livingston, 1982: 43–45). Members of these organizations embedded in a homophilous multiplex set of familial/kinship relations which socializes, reinforces and supports or even are aware of the terrorist organization, are far less likely to suffer disillusionment and burnout than those who are cut off from such supportive networks. Therefore it is far more likely that discrepant messages, alternative interpretations and diverse options will become visible and viable for organizational members who have begun to lose hope and remain cut off from their 'old' life. Such persons are also less likely to be resilient in the face of incarceration by the state and less willing, as they age, to accept the risk of returning to prison.

The successful creation of a backlash against terrorist and criminal organizations can also contribute to the burnout of organizational members, more particularly so those of terrorist organizational members who have entered the organization because they believe that they are operating on behalf of the community that is now reacting against them. Burnout is also more evident and more pronounced in ideological movements rather than ethno-nationalist movements because the community, until the original grievances are sufficiently ameliorated, are likely to be more supportive of the goal of the terrorist organization even while decrying their methods.

This suggests that the state needs to engage the community in the effort to isolate terrorists both from the organizations to which they have been connected and to assist in the process of questioning the methods by which terrorist goals are sought. If counterterrorism efforts become more successful, and the community also begins to generate a backlash against the terrorists, we may expect that there will be increased burnout among the members of the terrorist organization and an interest in departing before they are captured or killed. Horgan argues that in the case of the IRA, disengagement was very possible, and from an IRA organizational standpoint, very practical. One rule was: keep your mouth shut. The disengagement was very practical because the IRA believed that in the absence of a political solution there was a strong possibility that the member would return (see Horgan, 2009). The IRA thus made possible their leaving. But a key question is whether the state is also able to make that possible.

Let us suppose the terrorists have been weakened beyond hope, and alienated from their population. What follows? As doubt increases, hope of eventual success fades and the support of the community turns to opposition, it would be expected that individual members of the group will begin to search for alternatives and consider disengagement. In that search will they come across any alternatives that make that disengagement rational, any inducements that can be provided to them to walk away from the organization and/or for the organization to disband? In short, a restorative justice approach (rather than a retributive approach) might provide greater promise of community assistance in drawing out the more tightly knit and firmly embedded terrorists by promising opportunities for reintegration into the community and encourage a choice other than capture, victory or death. In that context, Cronin argues that offering an amnesty to members of a terrorist group is most likely to be successful where the organization is already facing defeat and its members see it as a losing cause (Cronin, 2006: 27).

If they cannot disengage without fear of continued pursuit by the state, what options might they pursue? Unfortunately, one option might be to seek to use their 'skills' in criminal activities and transform themselves and/or their organizations into strictly profit-making enterprises. This charge has been made with respect to the FARC (the revolutionary armed forces of Colombia) Thus, states might profitably consider the costs and benefits of programs that encourage reintegration of members of such organizations. If they do so, they will require very difficult discussions as to the level of crimes forgiven, including those that caused deaths. Closing off forgiveness or any level of leniency from those that have caused deaths will naturally reduce any incentive to disengage and thus even when it is clear that a cause is lost, members of the organization may continue to fight on and continue to cause civilian deaths. A clear example is the recent destruction of the Tamil Tigers of Sri Lanka. In the campaign that ended in May 2009, it is estimated that between 15,000 and 22,000 Tamil Tigers lost their lives, 275,000 civilians were displaced and 6,200 security personnel perished. While the government announced the defeat of the Tigers, some still suspect that surviving organizations may revive the Tigers at a later date (see BBC, 2010).

The other alternative of course is a continued strategy of incarceration with hopes of deradicalization and rehabilitation within the prison system. It has been argued that the success of rehabilitation will vary inversely with the extent of one's role within the illicit organization and that 'those engaged with violence are far less likely to be deradicalized or disengaged than supporters or members of logistic cells' (Abuja, 2009: 174). Rehabilitation is also less likely with a leader or central node within an organization. Prison systems have proven to be fertile recruiting grounds for terrorist organizations, converting criminal offenders into potential terrorists rather than rehabilitating offenders. Some effective deradicalization programs, while reducing the risk of a return to terrorist activities, have left untouched the risk of a return to criminal activities or continued support for the goals of the organization as may be the case in Indonesia (see Shultze, 2008). Nonetheless, the bargain appears to have overall positive returns given the relatively poor choices available to the Indonesian government. And perhaps that is an important if somewhat sobering conclusion. Governments and policy makers are often confronted with least bad rather than most good choices. In confronting intransigent and entrenched problems such as organized crime and terrorism, simple responses, even if consistently and forcefully applied cannot provide quick solutions. The problems of organized crime and terrorism have long histories and deep roots within the communities in which they have arisen. They require an approach that recognizes the history and context in which the problems and the organizations have emerged and builds upon the cooperation between communities and governments to begin meaningful and productive responses.

References

Abraham, I. and van Schendel, W. (2005) *Illicit Flows and Criminal Things: States, Borders, and the Other Side of Globalization*. Bloomington: Indiana University Press.

Arlacchi, P. and Calderone, A. (1992) *Men of Dishonor: Inside the Sicilian Mafia: An Account of Antonio Calderone*. New York: William Morrow & Co.

Australia, Department of Foreign Affairs and Trade (2006) 'Agreement between the Republic of Indonesia and Australia on the framework for security cooperation', http://www.dfat.gov.au/GEO/indonesia/ind-aus-sec06.html (accessed 5 July 2010).

Australian Federal Police (2008) 'The Street review: a review of interoperability between the AFP and its National Security Partners'. Australian Federal Police, Canberra. http://www.afp.gov.au/media-centre/~/media/afp/pdf/t/the-street-review.ashx (accessed 5 July 2010).

Ayling, J., P. Grabosky and C. Shearing (2009) *Lengthening the Arm of the Law: Enhancing Police Resources in the 21st Century*. Cambridge: Cambridge University Press.

Baker, P. (2009) 'Bush official, in book, tells of pressure on '04 vote', *The New York Times*, 20 August. http://www.nytimes.com/2009/08/21/us/21ridge.html?scp=2&sq=tom%20ridge&st=cse (accessed 5 July 2010).

Baker, W. and R. Faulkner (1993) 'The social organization of conspiracy: illegal networks in the heavy electrical equipment industry', *American Sociological Review*, 58: 837–860.

Ban, Ki-Moon (2007) 'Secretary General, at launch of "stolen asset recovery initiative", says measure is major step forward in collective efforts to address corruption', SG/SM/11161 UN Department of Public Information, News and Media Division, September 17.

Bayart, J.F., Ellis, S. and Hibou, B. (1999) *The Criminalization of the State in Africa*. Bloomington: Indiana University Press.

BBC News (2007) 'Madrid Train Attacks', http://news.bbc.co.uk/2/hi/in_depth/europe/2004/madrid_train_attacks/default.stm (accessed 5 July 2010).

BBC (2010) 'Tamil Tigers admit leader is dead', http://news.bbc.co.uk/2/hi/8066129.stm (accessed 5 July 2010).

Belur, J. (2009) 'Police use of deadly force: Police perceptions of a culture of approval', *Journal of Contemporary Criminal Justice*, 25 (2): 237–252.

Bennett, W., Lawrence, R. and Livingston, S. (2007) *When the Press Fails: Political Power and the News Media from Iraq to Katrina*. Chicago: University of Chicago Press.

Bjørgo, T. and Horgan, J. (eds) (2009) *Leaving Terrorism Behind: Individual and Collective Disengagement*. London: Routledge.

Bjornehed, E. (2004) 'Narco-terrorism: The merger of the war on drugs and the war on terror', *Global Crime*, 6 (3–4): 305–324.

Black, W. (2005) *The Best Way to Rob a Bank is to Own One: How Corporate Executives and Politicians Looted the S&L Industry*. Austin: University of Texas Press.

Blok, Anton (1975) *The Mafia of a Sicilian Village, 1860–1960: A Study of Violent Peasant Entrepreneurs*. New York: Harper and Row.

Boucek, C. (2009) 'Extremist re-education and rehabilitation in Saudi Arabia', in Bjørgo, T. and Horgan, J. (eds), *Leaving Terrorism Behind: Individual and Collective Disengagement*. Routledge, London. pp. 212–223.

Braun, S. (2007) 'Bad guys make even worse allies,' 13 August, *Los Angeles Times*. http://www.latimes.com/news/opinion/la-oe-braun13aug13,0,1196900. story?coll=la-opinion-center (accessed 5 July 2010).

Burton, F. (1978) *The Politics of Legitimacy: Struggles in a Belfast Community*. London: Routledge and Kegan Paul.

Bush, G.W. (2002) Remarks at presidential press conference March, 13. http://www.talkingpointsmemo.com/archives/149132.php (accessed 5 July 2010).

Bybee, J. (2002) Memorandum for Alberto R. Gonzales, Counsel to the President Re Standards of Conduct for Interrogation under 18 USC. ss2340-2340a. http://fl1.findlaw.com/news.findlaw.com/nytimes/docs/doj/bybee80102mem.pdf (accessed 5 July 2010).

Chu, Y. (2000) *The Triads as Business*. London: Routledge.

Claiborne, R. (1970) *Climate, Man and History*. New York: W.W. Norton and Co.

Clarke, R. and G. Newman (2006) *Outsmarting the Terrorists*. Westport: Praeger Security International.

Cohen, L. & Felson, M. (1979) 'Social change and crime rate trends: a routine activity approach'. *American Sociological Review*, 44 (4): 588–608.

Cohen, S (1996) 'Crime and politics: spot the difference', *The British Journal of Sociology*, 47 (1): 1–21.

Coll, S. (2004) *Ghost Wars: The Secret History of the CIA, Afghanistan, and Bin Laden, from the Soviet Invasion to September 10, 2001*. New York: Penguin Press.

Congressional Research Service (2006) Presidential Authority to Conduct Warrantless Electronic Surveillance to Gather Foreign Intelligence Information, http://www.fas.org/sgp/crs/intel/m010506.pdf (accessed 5 July 2010).

Congressional Research Service (2009) Renditions: Constraints Imposed by Laws on Torture. http://www.fas.org/sgp/crs/natsec/RL32890.pdf (accessed 5 July 2010).

Cowell, A. (1992) Sicilians Jeer Italian Leaders at a Funeral Protest, 22 July, *The New York Times*, http://query.nytimes.com/gst/fullpage.html?res=9E0CE0D6163CF931A15754C0A964958260 (accessed 5 July 2010).

Crenshaw, M. (1978) *Revolutionary Terrorism: The FLN in Algeria, 1954–1962*. Stanford, CA: Hoover Institution Press.

Cressey, D. (1969) *Theft of the Nation: The Structure and Operations of Organized Crime in America*. New York: Harper & Row.

Criminal Intelligence Service of Canada (2008) Report on Organized Crime, http://www.cisc.gc.ca/annual_reports/annual_report_2008/document/report_oc_2008_e.pdf (accessed 5 July 2010).

Cronin, A.K. (2006) 'How Al Qaeda Ends: The Decline and Demise of Terrorist Groups', *International Security*, 1: 7–48.

Cronin, A.K. (2009) *How Terrorism Ends: Understanding the Decline and Demise of Terrorist Campaigns*. Princeton: Princeton University Press.

Curtis, G. and T. Karacan (2002) 'The Nexus Between Terrorists, Narcotics Traffickers, Weapons Proliferators and Organized Crime Networks in Western Europe'. Library of Congress, Washington. http://www.loc.gov/rr/frd/pdf-files/WestEurope_NEXUS.pdf (accessed 5 July 2010).

Demaris, O. (1977) *Brothers in Blood: The International Terrorist Network*. New York: Scribners.

Denning, D. (2000) 'Cyberterrorism' Testimony before the Special Oversight Panel on Terrorism, Committee on Armed Services, US House of Representatives, 23 May. http://www.cs.georgetown.edu/~denning/infosec/cyberterror.html (accessed 5 July 2010).

Dishman, C. (2005) 'The leaderless nexus: when crime and terror converge', *Studies in Conflict and Terrorism*, 28: 237–252.

Donohue, L. (2008) *The Cost of Counterterrorism: Power, Politics and Liberty*. Cambridge: Cambridge University Press.

Dower, J. (1986) *War Without Mercy: Race and Power in the Pacific War*. New York: Pantheon Books.

Duvall, R. and Stohl, M. (1983) 'Governance by Terror' in Michael Stohl (ed.), *The Politics of Terrorism*, 2nd edition. New York: Marcel Dekker. pp. 179–220.

Ehrenfeld, R. (1987) 'Narco terrorism: The Kremlin Connection', Heritage Lecture #89. Available via http://www.heritage.org/Research/RussiaandEurasia/HL89.cfm. (accessed 5 July 2010).

Ellingwood, Ken (2009) 'Ciudad Juarez police chief quits after killings of officers, threats', *Los Angeles Times*, 21 February. http://www.latimes.com/news/nationworld/world/la-fg-mexico-police21-2009feb21,0,5260268.story (accessed 5 July 2010).

Enders, W. and T. Sandler (2005) 'After 9/11: is it all different now?', *The Journal of Conflict Resolution*, 49 (2): 259–277.

Erickson, B.H. (1981) 'Secret societies and social structure', *Social Forces*, 60, 188–210.

EUROPOL (2008) 'Organized Crime Threat Assessment'. The Hague: European Police Office.

Farrah, D. and S. Braun (2007) *Merchant of Death: Guns, Money Planes, and the Man Who Makes War Possible*. New York: John Wiley and Sons.

Fujimoto, T. (1998) 'Organized crime in Japan', *Comparative Law Review*, 32 (3): 1–22.

Gambetta, D. (1996) *The Sicilian Mafia: The Business of Private Protection*. Cambridge: Harvard University Press.

Gambetta, D. (ed.) (2005) *Making Sense of Suicide Missions*. Oxford: Oxford University Press.

Gamberra, D. (2009) *Codes of the Underworld: How Criminals Communicate*. Princeton: Princeton University Press.

Garrow, David (1981) *The FBI and Martin Luther King, Jr.* New York: W.W. Norton.

Gerth, H. and Mills, C. Wright (1958) *From Max Weber: Essays in Sociology*. New York: Oxford University Press.

Gilboy, J. (1998) 'Compelled third-party participation in the regulatory process: legal duties, culture and noncompliance', *Law and Policy*, 20: 135–155.

Glenny, M. (2008) *McMafia*. New York: Knopf.

Goldstock, R., Marcus, M., Thacher, T. and Jacobs, J. (1990) *Corruption and Racketeering in the New York City Construction Industry: The Final Report of the New York State Organized Task Force*. New York: New York University Press.

Gordon, S. (2009) 'Regionalism and cross-border cooperation against crime and terrorism in the Asia-Pacific', *Security Challenges*, 5 (4): 75–102.

Gurr, T. (1986) 'The political origins of state violence and terror: a theoretical analysis', in M. Stohl and G. Lopez (eds), *Government Violence and Repression: An Agenda for Research*. Westport, CT: Greenwood Press. pp. 45–71.

Grossman, H. and Noh, S. (1990) 'A theory of kleptocracy with probabilistic survival and reputation', *Economics & Politics*, 2 (2):157–171.

Haber, S. (ed.) (2002) *Crony Capitalism and Economic Growth in Latin America: Theory and Evidence.* Stanford CA: Hoover Institution Press.

Hacker, F. (1976) *Crusaders, Criminals, Crazies: Terror and Terrorism in our Time*. New York: W.W. Norton.

Hobbs, D. (2001) 'The firm: organizational logic and criminal culture on a shifting terrain', *British Journal of Criminology*, 41: 549–560.

Hoffman, B. (1998) *Inside Terrorism*. New York: Columbia University Press.

Hoffman, B. (2003) *Al Qaeda, Trends in Terrorism and Future Potentialities: An Assessment.* Santa Monica: Rand Corporation. http://www.rand.org/pubs/papers/P8078/P8078.pdf. (accessed 5 July 2010).

Horgan, John (2009) *Walking Away from Terrorism: Accounts of Disengagement from Radical and Extremist Movements.* London: Routledge.

Horne, A. (1977) *A Savage War of Peace: Algeria 1954–196.* London: Macmillan.

Huggins, M. (1991) 'US supported state terror: a history of police training in Latin America' in M. Huggins (ed.), *Vigilantism and the State in Modern Latin America: Essays on Extralegal Violence.* Westport, CT: Greenwood Publishing Group. pp. 219–242.

Hutchinson, S. and O'Malley, P. (2007) 'A crime terror nexus? Thinking on some of the links between terrorism and criminality,' *Studies in Conflict and Terrorism,* 30: 1095–1107.

Ianni, F. and Reuss-Ianni, E. (1972) *A Family Business: Kinship and Social Control in Organized Crime.* New York: Russell Sage Foundation.

Innes, M. (2004) 'Signal crimes and signal disorders: notes on deviance as communicative action', *British Journal of Sociology,* 55(3): 335-355.

Innes, M., Abbott, L., Lowe, T. and Roberts, C. (2007) *Hearts and Minds and Eyes and Ears: Reducing Radicalisation Risk Through Reassurance-oriented Policing.* Cardiff: Universities Police Science Institute.

International Crisis Group (2005) 'Zimbabwe's Operation Murambatsvina: The Tipping Point?', *Africa Report,* n97, 17 August. http://www.crisisgroup.org/~/media/Files/africa/southern-africa/zimbabwe/Zimbabwes%20Operation%20Murambatsvina%20The%20Tipping%20Point.ashx (accessed 5 July 2010).

Jacobs, J. (2006) *Mobsters, Unions and Feds: The Mafia and the American Labor Movement.* New York: New York University Press.

Jacobs, J. with Friel, C. and Radick, R. (1999) *Gotham Unbound: How New York City was Liberated from the Grip of Organized Crime.* New York: New York University Press.

Jenkins, B. (1975) 'International Terrorism: A New Mode of Conflict,' in David Carlton and Carlo Schaerf (eds), *International Terrorism and World Security.* London: Croom Helm.

Kaiser, D. (2008) *The Road to Dallas: The Assassination of John F. Kennedy.* Cambridge: Harvard University Press.

Kaplan, David. (2005) 'Paying for Terror: How Jihadist Groups are Using Organized Crime Tactics and Profits to Finance Attacks on Targets around the Globe.' *US News and World Report,* December 5, 2005. http://www.usnews.com/usnews/news/articles/051205/5terror.htm (accessed 6 July 2010).

Kaplan, D. and Dubro, A. (2003) *Yakuza: Japan's Criminal Underworld.* Berkeley: University of California Press.

Kazemian, L. and D. Farrington (eds) (2007) Special Issue, *Journal of Contemporary Criminal Justice,* 23 (4).

Kenney, M. (2007) *From Pablo to Osama: Trafficking and Terrorist Networks, Government Bureaucracies, and Competitive Adaptation*. University Park: The Pennsylvania State University Press.

Landesco, J. (1968) *Organized Crime in Chicago*. Chicago: University of Chicago Press.

Laub, J. and R. Sampson (2001) 'Understanding Desistance from Crime' in *Crime and Justice: an Annual Review of Research*. Chicago: University of Chicago Press. pp. 1–69.

Leo, R. (2008) *Police Interrogation and American Justice*. Cambridge, MA: Harvard University Press.

Levi, M. (2006) 'Organising serious, transnational and terrorist crimes', in M. Maguire, R. Morgan and R. Reiner (eds), *The Oxford Handbook of Criminology*, 4th edition. Oxford: Oxford University Press. Chapter 23.

Levi, M., Nelen, H. and Lankhorst, F. (2005) 'Lawyers as crime facilitators in Europe: An introduction and overview', *Crime, Law and Social Change*, 42 (2–3): 117–121.

Lichtblau, Eric (2005) 'Justice Dept. Defends Patriot Act Before Senate Hearings', *The New York Times*, 5 April. http://www.nytimes.com/2005/04/05/politics/05patriot.html (accessed 5 July 2010).

Lifton, R. (2000) *Destroying the World to Save It: Aum Shinrikyo, Apocalyptic Violence, and the New Global Terrorism*. New York: Henry Holt.

Lopez, G. A. (1986) 'National security ideology as an impetus to state violence and terror', in Michael Stohl and George Lopez (eds), *Government Violence and Repression: An Agenda for Research*. Westport, CT: Greenwood Press. pp. 73–96.

McIntosh, M. (1975) 'Changes in the organization of thieving', in S. Cohen (ed.), *Images of Deviance*. London: Penguin. pp. 98–133.

Maas, Peter (1968) *The Valachi Papers*. New York: Putnam.

Makarenko, T. (2004) 'The crime–terror continuum: tracing the interplay between transnational organised crime and terrorism', *Global Crime*, 6 (1): 129–145.

Mallory, S. (2007) *Understanding Organized Crime*. Sudbury, MA: Jones and Bartlett.

Marighela, C. (1971) *The Mini-Manual of the Urban Guerrilla*. London: Penguin.

Mayer, J. (2008) *The Dark Side: The Inside Story of How The War on Terror Turned into a War on American Ideals*. Doubleday, New York.

McCoy, A. (1972) *The Politics of Heroin in Southeast Asia: CIA Complicity in the Global Drug Trade*. New York: Harper and Row.

McGee, R. (2004) *The Philosophy of Taxation and Public Finance*. London: Kluwer Academic Publishers.

McGloin, Jean Marie (2005) 'Policy and intervention considerations of a network analysis of street gangs', *Criminology & Public Policy*, 4 (3): 607–635.

McSherry, P. (2002) 'Tracking the origins of a state terror network: Operation Condor', *Latin American Perspectives*, 29 (1): 38–60.

Merari, A., (2005) 'Social, organizational and psychological factors in suicide terrorism', in T. Bjørgo (ed.), *Root Causes of Terrorism*. New York: Routledge. pp. 70–86.

Merton, R. (1938) 'Social Structure and Anomie', *American Sociological Review*, 3 (6): 72–82.

Miller, A. and Damask, N. (1996) 'The dual myths of narco-terrorism: how myths drive policy', *Terrorism & Political Violence*, 8: 114–131.

Mincheva, L. and Gurr, T. (2010) 'Unholy Alliances: Ethnonationalism, International Crime, and the State in Post-Communist East Europe: The Case of Serbia.' Paper presented at the International Studies Association Annual Meeting, New Orleans, 17–20 February.

Mincheva, L. and Gurr, T. (In press; a) 'Unholy Alliances: How Trans-state Terrorism and International Crime Make Common Cause,' chapter 8 in Rafael Reuveny and William Thompson (eds), *Coping with Contemporary Terrorism: Origins, Escalation, Counter Strategies and Responses*. Albany, NY: State University of New York Press.

Mincheva, L. and Gurr, T. (In press; b) 'Unholy Alliances: Evidence on Linkages between Trans-State Terrorism and Crime Networks. The Case of Bosnia,' in Wolfgang Benedek, Christopher Daase, Petrus van Duyne, and Vojin Dimitrijevic (eds), *Transnational Terrorism, Organized Crime, and Peace-Building*. Palgrave Macmillan.

Ministry of Justice, Japan (2008) White Paper on Crime 2006. Research and Training Institute, Ministry of Justice, Tokyo.

Morgan, W.P. (1960) *Triad Societies in Hong Kong*. Hong Kong: Government Printer.

Morselli, C., Giguere, C. and Petit, K. (2007) 'The efficiency/security trade-off in criminal networks', *Social Networks*, 29: 143–153.

Morselli, Carlo (2009) *Inside Criminal Networks*. New York: Springer.

National Commission on Terrorist Attacks Upon the United States (2004) The 9/11 Commission Report. http://www.9-11commission.gov/report/911Report.pdf (accessed 11 August 2010).

Nikolić-Ristanovic, V. (1998) 'War and Crime in the former Yugoslavia', in V. Ruggiero, N. South and I. Taylor (eds), *New European Criminology*. London: Routledge. pp. 462–480.

Norton, A. (1988) 'Terrorism in the Middle East', in V. Pisano (ed.), *Terrorist Dynamics: A Geographical Perspective*. Arlington, VA: International Association of Chiefs of Police. pp. 1–44.

O'Brien, K. (2000) 'Truth and reconciliation in South Africa: Confronting the past, building the future?', *International Relations*, 15 (1): 1–16.

Ocampo, L. (2002) 'Building institutions: corruption and democracy. The Peruvian case of Montesinos', in *ReVista: Harvard Review of Latin America*, Fall 2002. http://www.drclas.harvard.edu/revista/articles/view/168

Ownby, David (2001) 'Recent Chinese Scholarship on the History of Chinese Secret Societies', *Late Imperial China*, 22 (1) June: 139–158.

Paoli, L. (2003) *Mafia Brotherhoods: Organized Crime Italian Style*. New York: Oxford University Press.

Pape, R. (2005) *Dying to Win: The Strategic Logic of Suicide Terrorism*. Chicago: University of Chicago Press.

Passas, N. (2006) 'Fighting terror with error: the counter-productive regulation of informal value transfers', *Crime, Law and Social Change*, 45 (4–5): 315–336.

Peceny, M. and Durnan, M. (2006) 'The FARC's Best Friend: US Antidrug Policies and the Deepening of Colombia's Civil War in the 1990s', *Latin American Politics and Society*, 48 (2): 95–116.

Perl, R. (2007) 'Combating Terrorism: The Challenge of Measuring Effectiveness', Report RL 33160, *Congressional Research Service*, March 12.

Pfeffer, J. and Salancik, G. (1978) *The External Control of Organizations: A Resource Dependence Perspective*. New York: Harper & Row.

Pickering, S., McCulloch, J. and Wright-Neville, D. (2008) *Counter-Terrorism Policing*. New York: Springer.

Pion-Berlin, D. (1989) *The Ideology of State Terror*. Boulder, CO: Lynne Rienner.

Pluchinsky, D. (2008) 'Global Jihadist Recidivism: A Red Flag', *Studies in Conflict and Terrorism*, 31 (3): 182–200.

Quinney, R. (1970) *The Social Reality of Crime*. Boston: Little Brown.

Rapoport, David (1992) 'Terrorism' in M. E. Hawkesworth and M. Kagan (eds), *Routledge Encyclopedia of Government and Politics*. London: Routledge. p. 1067.

Risen, James and Lichtblau, Eric (2005) 'Bush Lets US Spy on Callers Without Courts' *The New York Times*, 16 December. http://www.nytimes.com/2005/12/16/politics/16program.html?scp=3&sq=warrantless&st=nyt (accessed 5 July 2010).

Rock, P. (1977) 'Law, order and power in late seventeenth and early eighteenth century England', *Annales Internationales de Criminologie*, 16 (1–2): 233–265.

Ron, J. (1997) 'Varying methods of state violence', *International Organization*, 51 (2): 275–300.

Rosenthal, J. (2008) 'For-profit terrorism: the rise of armed entrepreneurs', *Studies in Conflict and Terrorism*, 31 (6): 481–498.

Ross, J.I. and Gurr, T. R. (1989) 'Why terrorism subsides: a comparative study of Canada and the United States', *Comparative Politics*, 21 (4): 405–426.

Rummel, R. (2007) 'Statistics of democide: genocide and mass murder since 1900', Charlottesville, Virginia: Center for National Security Law, School of Law, University of Virginia, 1997; and Transaction Publishers, Rutgers University.

Russell, C., & Miller, B. (1977) 'Profile of a terrorist', *Terrorism*, 1: 17–34.

Sageman, M. (2008) *Leaderless Jihad*. Philadelphia: University of Pennsylvania Press.

Sanderson, T. (2004) 'Transnational terror and organized crime: blurring the lines', *SAIS Review*, 24 (1): 49–64.

Scherer, M. (2004) 'Dealing with the merchant of death' *Mother Jones*, September 20. http://www.globalpolicy.org/component/content/article/165/29529.html (accessed 5 July 2010).

Schloenhardt, Andreas (2009) Palermo on the Pacific Rim: Organized crime Offences in the Asia-Pacific Region. UN Office of Drugs and Crime, Vienna. http://www.unodc.org/documents/eastasiaandpacific//2009/08/Palermo/Schloenhardt_Palermo_in_the_Pacific_07_Final_UNODC_2009.pdf (accessed 11 August 2010).

Schmid, A. (1996) 'Links between transnational organized crime and terrorist crimes', *Transnational Organized Crime*, 2 (4): 40–82.

Schneider, Jane and Schneider, Peter (2002) 'The Mafia and al-Qaeda: violent and secretive organizations in comparative and historical perspective', *American Anthropologist*, 104 (3): 776–782.

Scott, J.C. (1969) 'Corruption, Machine Politics and Political Change', *American Political Science Review*, 63 (4): 1142–1158.

Serious Organized Crime Agency (SOCA) (2008) UK Threat Assessment of Serious Organised Crime 2008/9. http://www.soca.gov.uk/assess Publications/UKTA0809.html (accessed 2 February 2009).

Sipress, A. (2004) 'An Indonesian's prison memoir takes Holy War into cyberspace': In Sign of New Threat, Militant Offers Tips on Credit Card Fraud, *Washington Post*, December 14, A19. http://msl1.mit.edu/furdlog/docs/washpost/2004-12-14_washpost_jihadis_online.pdf (accessed 5 July 2010).

Sterling, C. (1981) *The Terror Network*. New York: Holt, Rinehart and Winston.

Stern, J. (2003) *Terror in the Name of God: Why Religious Militants Kill*. New York: Harper Collins.

Stern, J. (2006) 'Jihad: a global fad', *The Boston Globe*, August 1. http://www.boston.com/news/world/middleeast/articles/2006/08/01/jihad_a_global_fad/ (accessed 5 July 2010).

Stohl, M. (1983) 'The International Network of Terrorism', *Journal of Peace Research*, 20 (1): 59–66.

Stohl, M. (1998) 'Demystifying terrorism: the myths and realities of contemporary terrorism', in M. Stohl (ed.), *The Politics of Terrorism*. New York: Marcel Dekker. pp. 1–19.

Stohl, M. (2006) 'The state as terrorist: insights and implications', *Democracy and Security*, 2: 1–25.

Stohl, C. and Stohl, M. (2007) 'Networks of terror: theoretical assumptions and pragmatic consequences', *Communication Theory*, 17 (2): 93–124.

Stohl, M., D. Carleton and S. Johnson (1984) 'Human rights and US foreign assistance from Nixon to Carter', *Journal of Peace Research*, 3: 1–11.

Sutherland, E.H. and Cressey, D.R. (1947) *Principles of Criminology*, 4th edition. Philadelphia: J. B. Lippincott.

Szabo, Stephen (ed.) (1983) *The Successor Generation: International Perspectives of Postwar Europeans*. London: Butterworths.

Thacher, D. (2005) 'The Local Role in Homeland Security', *Law and Society Review*, 39 (3): 635–676.

Tilly, C. (1975) 'Reflections on the History of European State-Making', in Charles Tilly (ed.), *The Formation of National States in Western Europe*. Princeton, NJ: Princeton University Press. p. 42.

Tilly, C. (1985) 'War Making and State Making as Organized Crime', in Peter Evans, Dietrich Rueschemeyer and Theda Skocpol (eds), *Bringing the State Back In*. Cambridge: Cambridge University Press. pp. 169–191.

Treverton, G., Matthies, C., Cunningham, C., Goulka, J., Ridgeway,G. and A. Wong (2009) *Film Piracy, Organized Crime and Terrorism*. Santa Monica, CA: RAND Corporation.

Tuchman, B.(1978) *A Distant Mirror: The Calamitous 14th Century*. New York: Knopf.

United Nations (2008) UN Action to Counter Terrorism. http://www.un.org/terrorism/ (accessed 15 December 2008).

United Nations, Office of Drugs and Crime (2009) World Drug Report 2009, Executive Summary. http://www.unodc.org/documents/wdr/WDR_2009/Executive_summary_LO-RES.pdf (accessed 5 July 2010).

US Congress (1987) 'Report of the Congressional Committees Investigating the Iran-Contra Affair (S. Rep. No. 216, H.R. Rep. No. 433, 100th Cong., 1st Sess.)'. Washington: United States Government Printing Office.

Van Gennep, A. (1909) *Les Rites de Passage*. Étude Systématique des rites. Paris: E Nourry.

Williams, P. (1999) 'Transnational criminal networks', in J. Arquilla and D. Ronfeldt (eds), *Networks and Netwars*. Santa Monica: Rand. pp. 61–97.

Williams, P. (2001) 'Transnational Criminal Networks' in John Arquilla and David Ronfeldt (eds), *Networks and Netwars: The Future of Terror, Crime and Militancy*. RAND Corporation, Santa Monica. pp. 65–97.

Williams, P. (2001) 'Crime, illicit markets, and money laundering in managing global issues lessons learned', in Chantal de Jonge Oudraat and P.J. Simmons (eds), *Managing Global Issues: Lessons Learned*. Carnegie Endowment for International Peace. pp. 106–150.

Wolfe, T. (1970) *Radical Chic and Mau Mauing the Flak Catchers*. New York: Farrar, Straus and Giroux.

Worth, R. (2009a) Freed by the US, Saudi Becomes a Qaeda Chief. *New York Times*, 22 January, http://www.nytimes.com/2009/01/23/world/middleeast/23yemen.html (accessed 5 July 2010).

Worth, R. (2009b) Alumni of Saudi Program for Ex-Jihadists Are Arrested. *New York Times*, 26 January, http://www.nytimes.com/2009/01/27/world/middleeast/27saudi.html (accessed 5 July 2010).

Zawahiri, A. (2005) Letter from al-Zawahiri to al-Zarqawi, http://www.globalsecurity.org/security/library/report/2005/zawahiri-zarqawi-letter_9jul2005.htm (accessed 5 July 2010).

Zoepf, K. (2008) 'Deprogramming Jihadists' *The New York Times Magazine*, November, 9: 50–53.

Index

Page references in *italics* indicate boxes and those in **bold** indicate tables.

hawala 48, 102
Hell's Angels (Canada) 111
Hezbollah (Lebanon) 6, 17,
        53, 64, 75–76, 84
Hobbs, Dick 30n4
Hoffman, Bruce 81
homophily 84–85, 125
Hoover, J. Edgar 106
Horgan, John 125
human trafficking 35, **36**, 49
Hutchinson, Steven 7–8, 85

Ianni, Francis 30n4
Ibrahim, Dawood 77, 78
Idi Amin regime (Uganda) 52
India 4, 48
    see also D-Company (India)
Indonesia 7, 48, 109, 127
    counterterrorism and 92
information flow 23–24, 93
initiation ceremonies 21
Innes, Martin 10, 12, 21, 22
intellectual property piracy 49
intelligence 93–94
interception of telecommunications
        93–94, 96–97
International Terrorism 41
Internet 39, 96
Iran 53, 55, 61, 64
Iran-Contra affair 49, 53, 67–68
Iraq 46, 89, 117
Irgun (Israel) 111
Irish Republican Army (IRA)
    bank robberies 7
    decline and political settlement
        5, 46, 111, 113, 117
Irish Republican Army (IRA)
    disengagement 125
    fundraising 47
    initiation ceremonies 22
Islamic Movement of
        Uzbekistan (IMU) 76
Israel 111
Italy
    Albanian refugees and 50
    assassinations of Falcone
        and Borsellino 6–7, 77,
        108, *108–109*, 121
    organized crime 15

Italy *cont.*
    Red Brigades (Italy) 48, 112–113
    see also Mafia (Italy)
ITERATE 41, 43, *43*, 45, *46*

Jacobs, James 17, 105
Janjalani, Abdurajak Abubakar 76
Japan 32, 78
    see also Aum Shinrikyo (Japan);
        Yakuza organizations (Japan)
Japanese Red Army 75
Jemaah Islamiyah (JI,
        Indonesia) 7, 94
Jenkins, Brian 45, 64
jihad 39, 48, 116
Johnson administration 88–89

Kaczynski, Theodore
        (Unabomber) 37
Kaplan, David 75
Kashmir 6, 64, 77
Kelly, Ned 26
Kennedy administration 25–26,
        88–89, 106
Kenney, Michael 16, 18–19, 23
kidnappings 6, 36–37, 48, 76–77
King, Martin Luther, Jr. 106
kleptocracy 56
Kosovo Liberation Army 85
Krueger, Alan B. 42n5
Kurdistan Workers' Party 117

Laitin, David D. 42n5
Langan, Peter 75
Lashkar-e-Taiba (LET,
        Pakistan) 64, 77
Lazarenko, Pavlo 57
leaders and leadership
        19, 114–119
Lebanon *see* Hezbollah (Lebanon)
legislation 25, 99–104
Letelier, Orlando 55
Liberation Tigers of Tamil Eelam
        (Sri Lanka) 5, 48, 49, 113, 126
Liberia 56, 68–69
Libya 6, 52–53, 55, 61
Lifton, Robert Jay 22
loan sharking 11
Lockerbie bombing 6, 52